BACK
TO
WORK

TESTING
REEMPLOYMENT SERVICES
FOR
DISPLACED WORKERS

Howard S. Bloom
New York University

1990

W.E. UPJOHN INSTITUTE for Employment Research
Kalamazoo, Michigan

Library of Congress Cataloging-in-Publication Data

Bloom, Howard S.
   Back to work : testing reemployment services for displaced workers
 /   Howard S. Bloom.
        p.   cm.
   Includes bibliographical references and index.
   ISBN 0-88099-097-X (alk. paper). — ISBN 0-88099-098-8 (pbk. :
 alk. paper)
   1. Displaced workers—Services for—Texas—Case studies.
 2. Unemployed—Services for—Texas—Case studies. 3. Employment
 agencies—Texas—Case studies. 4. Occupational retraining—Texas—
 Case studies.   I. Title.
 HD5725.T5B55   1990
 331.12'8—dc20   90-12909
                                                                         CIP

Copyright © 1990
W. E. Upjohn Institute for Employment Research
300 S. Westnedge Avenue
Kalamazoo, Michigan 49007

The facts presented in this study and the observations and viewpoints expressed are the sole responsibility of the author. They do not necessarily represent positions of the W. E. Upjohn Institute for Employment Research.

Printed in the U.S.A.

Preface

During the past decade, millions of American workers have lost stable, well-paying jobs due to structural economic changes caused by major advances in production technology and rapidly increasing international competition. These displaced workers often remained unemployed for long periods of time, and when they finally become reemployed, it was frequently in jobs that paid less than those that were lost.

Estimates of the magnitude of this problem during the early 1980s varied from roughly 200,000 to two million workers a year, or 1 to 20 percent of the unemployed (Bendick and Devine 1981; Sheingold 1982). More recent estimates place the number of displaced workers at about one million per year, or 10 percent of the unemployed (Flaim and Sehgal 1985).

The primary national response to this problem was passage of Title III of the Job Training Partnership Act (JTPA), which became law in October 1982 and took effect in October 1983. This federal program currently serves roughly 100,000 persons annually, or 10 percent of the nation's displaced workers (U.S. Department of Labor 1988). Roughly $200 million is spent each year (U.S. General Accounting Office 1990) for programs funded by the federal government, administered mainly by the states, and provided by a broad array of public, private, and not-for-profit organizations.

Title III programs combine approaches geared to immediate reemployment through job-search assistance with longer-range strategies to increase human capital through occupational skills training. In program year 1987, about 38 percent of all participants received job-search assistance, 28 percent received classroom training, 19 percent received on-the-job training, and 15 percent received other services (U.S. Department of Labor 1988).

In the early 1980s, when Title III was being implemented, little was known about the problems of displaced workers and how best to assist them. It had been two decades since the nation had focused on worker displacement (very briefly, in the initial years of the 1962 Manpower Development and Training Act), and there was little in the way of program experience or research findings to help direct this major federal initiative. Hence, funds were made available to the states, but there was very little guidance for the use of these funds.

To help fill this knowledge gap, a forward-thinking and innovative group at the Texas Department of Community Affairs embarked on a demonstration program to study the design, implementation, impacts and costs of a combination of job-search assistance and occupational skills training for displaced workers. This project, the Texas Worker Adjustment Demonstration, successfully implemented a large, rigorous, randomized experimental evaluation in three sites.

From this experience much was learned about institutional arrangements for displaced worker programs, alternative methods for recruiting participants, program-intake effects on participation, factors influencing the types of services provided and received, impacts on future earnings, employment, and unemployment insurance benefits, and the costs of providing services.

As with any single research study, findings from the Texas Worker Adjustment Demonstration are suggestive, not definitive. They indicate probable fruitful options, but do not prove specific points. Nevertheless, this project represents a large portion of the small research base that exists on a problem of major national significance.

We now are entering a new stage of displaced worker programming, with the onset of the Economic Dislocation and Worker Adjustment Assistance Act of 1988 (EDWAA). Based on past research, program experience, and expert judgment (e.g., the Secretary of Labor's Task Force on Economic Adjustment and Worker Dislocation 1986), EDWAA is attempting to change the funding, the state and local institutional structure, the target-group focus, and the service mix of federally-funded displaced-worker programs. In addition, local economic displacement caused by potential reductions in the military budget reflecting attempts to produce a *peace dividend* may substantially increase the need for displaced worker programs in some localities (U.S. Congressional Budget Office 1990).

Once again, however, state and local governments are being asked to consider major new initiatives with a minimum of guidance and a modest research base to draw on. It is hoped that the present volume will contribute specific information to this effort, and stimulate further rigorous testing of innovations so that future programs can make better use of past experience.

Acknowledgements

This monograph is based on the author's experience as principal investigator for the Texas Worker Adjustment Demonstration. The project was commissioned and funded by the Texas Department of Community Affairs (TDCA). It was a rigorously designed and carefully implemented randomized field experiment to study the implementation, impacts, and costs of job-search assistance and retraining services for displaced workers.

The demonstration was evaluated by Abt Associates, Inc. of Cambridge, Massachusetts, under contract to TDCA. Evaluation findings were presented in four reports: Bloom, Kulik, Schneider, and Sharpe 1984; Jastrzab, Kulik, Schneider, and Sharpe 1984; Kulik and Sharpe 1985; Bloom and Kulik 1986. Findings in this monograph are based on the original evaluation data, but differ slightly from those in project reports due to subsequent analytic modifications.

All major research projects reflect the effort of many persons and the current study was no exception. Of particular importance were members of the Abt Associates, Inc. team who conducted the evaluation, TDCA staff who developed and supported the project, and local site personnel who made the demonstration a reality.

Project director for the Abt team was Jane Kulik, who had overall administrative responsibility for the evaluation and directed the program implementation and cost studies. Other team members were Linda Sharpe, senior on-site analyst and project coordinator; JoAnn Jastrzab, data collection manager; Glen Schneider, site development specialist and project facilitator; Robert Sharik, data-base developer and manager; Ellen Lee, computer programmer; Wanda Ford and Juan Montes, on-site analysts; and Geri and Bill Keigh, survey subcontractors.

Christopher T. King, TDCA Assistant Director for Research, Development, and Evaluation at the time, directed the state staff that conceived and promoted the demonstration. Mary Jane Leahy, project officer for the demonstration, was central to both its development and completion. Saundra Kirk, project liaison, played a key role in its initial implementation.

Local project directors were Jean Wood for the Texas Employment Commission/Houston Community College consortium, Iris Burnham for the School for Educational Enrichment project in El Paso, and Ruben Villalobos for the SER Jobs for Progress project in El Paso.

The fact that this monograph was actually written is due to support from the W. E. Upjohn Institute for Employment Research and the patience of its Assistant Executive Director, Dr. H. Allan Hunt. Also critical to this final stage was the assistance of Christopher T. King, Judith Gentry, Jane Kulik, Steve Albert, and Elizabeth Sherman, who reviewed the entire manuscript, and Hans Bos, who produced the graphics.

The Author

Howard S. Bloom is Director of Doctoral Studies for the Robert F. Wagner Graduate School of Public Service at New York University. Professor Bloom is an evaluation research methodologist and has published numerous studies of employment and training programs. He was co-author of a national evaluation of CETA for the U.S. Congressional Budget Office and the National Commission for Employment Policy. Currently he is co-principal investigator for the National JTPA Study, one of the largest randomized field experiments ever conducted in the social sciences.

Summary

Back to Work: Testing Reemployment Services for Displaced Workers presents lessons learned from the Texas Worker Adjustment Demonstration, a 2,192-person randomized experimental evaluation of reemployment programs for displaced workers conducted at three Texas sites during 1984–85. This project demonstrated that a relatively inexpensive mix of job-search assistance and limited occupational skills training can be a cost-effective means of assisting *some* displaced workers. In addition, it demonstrated the feasibility of conducting a high-quality, randomized field experiment at several sites simultaneously, within a modest budget and limited time frame.

The monograph describes in detail: (1) the background, design, conduct, and content of the programs at each demonstration site; (2) the evaluation design, implementation process, data collection effort, and analysis; (3) factors that influenced participation in the program, with special emphasis on characteristics of the program intake process, participants' backgrounds, and available program services; (4) program impacts for men and for women, as well as other key subgroups, in terms of their future earnings, employment, and unemployment insurance (UI) benefits; and (5) program costs. This information should be of interest to policymakers and managers who must design and operate future displaced worker programs, and researchers who wish to study these and other social programs.

Key findings from the study are as follows:

(1) Program impacts for displaced female workers were substantial and sustained throughout the one-year follow-up period, although they diminished continually over time. Female participants experienced a $1,148 or 34 percent average annual *program-induced* earnings gain, and at the end of the follow-up period their weekly earnings were 19 percent higher than they would have been in the absence of the program. Correspondingly, female participants received $227 or 19 percent less in UI benefits during their first 30 weeks after entering the program. There was little remaining margin for further benefit reductions, since most benefit entitlements were exhausted by this time.

(2) Impacts for men were appreciable, but much smaller and shorter-lived than those for women. Male participants experienced an average annual program-induced earnings gain of $673 or 8 percent, almost all of which occurred soon after they entered the program. This early and brief reemployment boost reduced UI benefits by $207 per male participant or 13 percent.

(3) Average costs per participant were $725 and $1,099 at the two sites that were most comparable to the corresponding Title III national average, $904. Hence, measured earnings impacts for women (which were based only on these two sites) exceeded their program costs. In addition, because earnings impacts for women appeared to continue beyond the follow-up period, their net positive balance was probably greater than that measured. Furthermore, because reduced UI benefits represent an offset to government program costs, the cost-effectiveness picture for women was even more favorable from the government's budgetary perspective. For men at these two sites, however, earnings impacts were slightly less than program costs. But when UI benefit reductions were considered, the programs roughly *broke even*.

The third demonstration site conducted a more elaborate program, costing between $2,981 and $3,381 per participant. Program impacts for men were about the same as those for the other two sites and thus were much less than program costs. Impacts for women were not reported because of sample size limitations.

Contents

Part I: Background

Part II: Findings

Tables

Figures

Part I

Background

The four chapters in this section provide an historical, institutional, and methodological framework for interpreting findings from the Texas Worker Adjustment Demonstration. Chapter 1 outlines the genesis and implementation of the demonstration and the roles played by the key organizations involved. Chapter 2 presents the evaluation design and methodology. Chapter 3 describes the data used for the evaluation. Chapter 4 describes the sample of individuals whose experiences provide the basis for the analysis.

1
The Demonstration

This chapter presents the background and describes the operation of the Worker Adjustment Demonstration. Specifically, it discusses the policy framework and issues that gave rise to the demonstration, describes how each site operated, outlines the roles of the project sponsor and evaluation contractor, and describes the local economic environment in which the demonstration was conducted.

The Problem and the Project

Between October 1983—when the Job Training Partnership Act (JTPA) took effect—and June 1986—the end of its third year—over $421 million was appropriated for displaced worker programs under JTPA Title III. Nationally, over 700 programs were providing retraining and reemployment assistance to tens of thousands of persons who each year had lost well-paying, stable jobs due to changing technology and increased international competition. Nevertheless, little was known about the implementation, effectiveness, or costs of these programs.

To help bridge this information gap, the Texas Department of Community Affairs (TDCA) conducted an innovative Worker Adjustment Demonstration. This project had two primary objectives:

1. To expedite reemployment for displaced workers in stable, productive jobs that minimized their wage loss
2. To provide planners of future Title III programs with insights into factors affecting the design, implementation, operation, cost, and success of their programs

The Worker Adjustment Demonstration was based on a two-tier service model that required all participants to complete a period of assisted job-search—Tier I—prior to consideration for additional reemployment or retraining services—Tier II. This strategy reflected the premise that many displaced workers could be reemployed through job-search assistance. By doing so, it was hoped that more intensive services could be reserved for persons who most needed them.

To test these and related propositions, TDCA conducted the Worker Adjustment Demonstration as a randomized experiment. A comprehensive evaluation of the demonstration was conducted to address the following questions:

> How was the demonstration planned, implemented, and operated? How did it vary across sites? How were these variations related to differences in local economic conditions, population characteristics, and institutional arrangements? What were the key problems incurred, and how might these problems be avoided in the future?

> What types of persons participated in the program? How did program services differ by type of participant? How were differences across sites related to their industrial and occupational mix, the nature and source of their economic displacement, and the types of community services that were available?

> What was the program's impact on future employment, earnings and Unemployment Insurance (UI) benefits? How did this impact vary by type of participant? To what extent, if any, did retraining add to the impact of job-search assistance, and what were the costs of services provided?

Phase 1 of the demonstration began in 1983, with a TDCA request for proposals to conduct local programs in targeted areas throughout Texas. After carefully reviewing proposals, the State Job Training Coordinating Council (SJTCC) recommended to the governor that three projects be funded:[1]

1. A $1,089,700 project operated by the Texas Employment Commission (TEC) and Houston Community College (HCC)—(TEC/HCC);
2. A $763,400 project operated by Programs for Human Services (PHS), a community-based organization serving Beaumont/Orange/Port Arthur; and

3. A $903,500 project operated by the Cameron County Private Industry Council.[2]

These projects were funded in November 1983, from a combination of Emergency Jobs Bill monies and the transition year 1983 JTPA Title III Grant.[3] They were operated through June 1984, but were not subject to a comprehensive evaluation.[4]

Phase 2 of the demonstration involved five projects funded by the program year 1984 JTPA Title III Grant. Two of these projects were continuations from Phase 1.

1. A $1,425,000 extension of the TEC/HCC program in Houston.
2. A $950,000 extension of the PHS program in Beaumont/ Orange/Port Arthur.

In addition, three new initiatives were selected:

1. A $288,000 project operated by the El Paso School for Educational Enrichment (SEE), a private education and training organization;
2. A $295,000 project operated by Greater El Paso SER Jobs for Progress (SER/JOBS), a local unit of the well-known national community-based employment and training organization; and
3. A $685,000 project operated by Vocational Guidance Services (VGS), a community-based organization serving the Galveston area.

These projects were selected through a competition that also included proposals from five other parts of the state. Given the limited funds available for the demonstration, each proposal was screened carefully. Final selections were based on the quality of proposals received and the extent to which key industries identified by the state were particularly hard hit in each locality. Phase 2 projects began between May and July of 1984, and ran for approximately one year. In contrast to Phase 1, the second group of projects included a comprehensive evaluation, and each project was chosen on the condition that it participate in the evaluation.

The evaluation contractor, Abt Associates, Inc. of Cambridge, Massachusetts, was selected through a competition in 1984, soon after the Phase 2 projects were chosen. Thus, even though the Phase 2 projects were willing to implement an evaluation, they could not fully appreciate the implications of doing so until after the evaluation contractor was chosen and the evaluation design was developed. This, in turn, complicated the evaluation contractor's initial task. Nevertheless, after a series of site meetings and planning sessions, evaluation designs were agreed upon by each site. These were fashioned to provide the information required by TDCA and to accommodate the conditions and constraints at each site.

The evaluation plan (Bloom et al. 1984) involved a randomized experiment at each site, undertaken to measure program impacts on future earnings, employment, and UI benefits. This approach, whereby eligible program applicants were randomly assigned to treatment groups who were offered program services or control groups who were not, represents the most powerful existing methodology for measuring the impacts of social programs (Riecken and Boruch 1974; Hausman and Wise 1985). Furthermore, given the limited existing resources, relative to the widespread need for assistance, random selection of eligible applicants by lottery was the fairest possible way to allocate program services.

The evaluation plan also included detailed case studies of how each program was implemented, what problems arose, how these problems were addressed, and how the programs operated. Thus, the evaluation was designed to provide information that would facilitate interpretation of impact results and inform future efforts to implement displaced worker programs. The evaluation plan also included an analysis of program costs, undertaken to develop cost-effectiveness measures.

Soon after Phase 2 began, PHS in Beaumont/Orange/Port Arthur, and VGS in Galveston, dropped out of the impact evaluation. PHS dropped out when several major alternative sources of reemployment assistance became available, in response to the areas's rapidly deepening economic crisis.[5] These resources made equivalent program services available to control group members. VGS dropped out of the evaluation when management problems and conflicts with its initial applicant source became insurmountable.

Nevertheless, three of the five Phase 2 demonstration sites—TEC/HCC, SEE, and SER/JOBS—ran to completion. These sites provide the basis for the discussion that follows.

The Programs

TEC/HCC, SEE and SER/JOBS developed and implemented worker adjustment programs that reflected a number of factors, including: the economic conditions they faced; their institutional histories, missions, and positions in the community; the services with which they had the most experience; their management and staff preferences; responses to specific problems and opportunities that arose; and external forces.

Program Organization

Sites were required by TDCA to operate a generic two-tier job-search assistance and retraining program within certain specified parameters. Table 1.1 illustrates how this program model was adopted and adapted.

Table 1.1
Program Administration

	TEC/HCC	SEE	SER/JOBS
Contractor type	Public	For-profit	Not-for-profit
Phase 1 contractor	Yes	No	No
Contract amount	$1,425,000	$288,000	$295,000
Contract period	7/84 to 7/85	4/84 to 3/85	4/84 to 3/85
Assignment period	7/84 to 2/85	6/84 to 2/85	8/84 to 2/85
Planned sample			
Tier I only	250	---	---
Tier I/II	350	250	250
Tier II	200	125	125

Each program was directed by a different type of organization. TEC and HCC were public agencies, SER/JOBS was a private not-for-profit community-based organization, and SEE was a private for-profit vocational education institution. Although the contract period for all three programs was one year, their funding levels varied from $1,425,000 for TEC/HCC to $288,000 and $295,000 for SEE and SER/JOBS, respectively. Consequently, their activity levels varied substantially.

TEC/HCC planned two alternative program strategies, or treatment streams. One treatment stream, Tier I only, was designed to provide job-search assistance to 250 persons. The second treatment stream, Tier I/II, was designed to serve 350 persons. All Tier I/II participants were to start with job-search assistance. Subsequently, about 200 were expected to receive classroom training or on-the-job training (OJT).[6]

Both SEE and SER/JOBS planned a single Tier I/II program of job-search assistance for all participants, followed by occupational skills training for some. SEE and SER/JOBS each planned to serve 250 persons, half of whom were expected to receive classroom training or OJT. Table 1.2 presents an overview of the major components of the demonstration programs at each site and the following sections briefly describe these components.

Client Recruitment

Program applicants were recruited from three sources:

1. UI claimants referred by TEC
2. Walk-ins generated by publicity and word of mouth
3. Plant-based outreach to mass layoffs

The overwhelming majority of applicants were recruited through UI claimant referrals; little recruitment was accomplished through walk-ins or plant-specific outreach.

TEC/HCC recruited all of its applicants internally. The first step in this process was a brief application interview at a local TEC unemployment insurance office. Four Houston TEC offices were designated for this purpose. The second step was an orientation session at the TEC/HCC

Table 1.2
Program Overview

	TEC/HCC	SEE	SER/JOBS
Intake	TEC referrals by •TEC office •industry •occupation	•TEC referrals by industry •Plant-based outreach •Walk-ins	•TEC referrals •Plant-based outreach •Walk-ins
Assessment			
Occupational	Yes	Yes	No
Educational	No	Yes	No
Tier I			
Job search			
Days	5 (Career circles)	5	5
Hours/day	6	4	4
Days	5 (TEC)	--	--
Hours/day	4	--	--
Job club			
Recommended	Daily for 4 weeks	Weekly for 3 weeks	Daily
Required	Once weekly	None	None
Tier II			
Classroom training	Air conditioning Computer maintenance Computer command technology Computer drafting	Clerical Bookkeeping English	Clerical Auto mechanics English
OJT	Yes	Yes	Yes
Support services			
Transportation	$5/day for Tier 1	$1/day	$15 attendance reward
Child care	Yes	Not used	Not used

demonstration headquarters. Because it had a large internal base of applicant referrals, TEC/HCC did not experience serious recruitment problems.

SEE initially focused recruitment on workers who had been laid off from an Atari assembly plant and a Calvin Klein warehouse. Other smaller plants also were targeted, but despite these efforts, as well as referrals from the Texas Rehabilitation Commission and the Adult Parole Board, SEE needed to augment its referral pool. Consequently, it sought help from TDCA to contract with the El Paso TEC office for UI claimant referrals from specified industries. SER/JOBS's initial recruitment strategy relied on advertising and word of mouth, but these produced few enrollments. Thus, SER/JOBS also requested that TDCA contract with the El Paso TEC for UI claimant referrals.

Client Targeting

Eligibility criteria for the demonstration required that applicants be in one of the following categories:

1. Unemployed with a poor chance of returning to work, as evidenced, for example, by a permanent plant shutdown or long-term layoff unrelated to regular cyclical activity;
2. Recipients of Unemployment Insurance benefits or benefit exhaustees;
3. Faced with special barriers to reemployment, such as being an older worker or not speaking English.

These general criteria reflected TDCA's interpretation of JTPA Title III requirements.[7] Sites also had specific guidelines (table 1.3) based on analyses of labor market information and other economic data. For example, TEC/HCC focused on petrochemicals, steel, shipbuilding and repair, refining, oil and gas extraction, and chemical processing. Within these industries, certain occupations were emphasized, e.g., engineering, management, clerical/sales, machine trades, and processing. SEE and SER/JOBS emphasized certain industries but not specific occupations.

TEC referred workers from the four of its nine Houston offices nearest to concentrations of its target groups. The location of these offices, plus

Table 1.3
Client Recruitment Criteria

	TEC/HCC	SEE	SER/JOBS
Target industries	Petrochemicals	Apparel	Food
	Steel	Retail	Clothing
	Shipbuilding	Electronics	Construction
	Refining	Wholesale	Chemical
	Oil and gas	Manufacturing	Mining
	Chemical	Construction	Electronics
		Health service	Smelting
		Chemical	Retail/wholesale
			Trucking/freight
Target occupations	Machinist	None[a]	None[a]
	Drafter		
	Mechanical engineer		
	Engineering technician		
	Accountant		
	Civil engineer		
	Financial analyst		
	Purchasing agent		
	Geologist		
	Arc welder		
	Crane operator		
	Quality control		
	Economist		
	Electrical repair		
	Field engineer		
UI status	Claimants and exhaustees	Mainly claimants 6+ weeks	Mainly claimants 8 – 13 weeks
Language	English	English primarily	English or Spanish

a. Original demonstration plans specified that all sites identify target occupations, but SEE and SER/JOBS did not implement this feature.

the recruitment criteria applied, produced a mostly white-collar demonstration sample. SEE initially followed a plant-based recruitment strategy focused on laid-off apparel and electronics workers. Subsequently, this effort was augmented by UI claimant referrals. SER/JOBS also had to rely heavily on this applicant source.

To deal with disparities in language backgrounds, SEE established separate classes for English- and Spanish-speaking participants. SER/JOBS filled classes on a first-come, first-served basis and taught them in the language spoken by the majority of participants.

Targeting at all sites was influenced by a powerful financial incentive to enroll current UI claimants. This pressure was created by TDCA's decision to pass the JTPA Title III resource-matching requirement through to each site. By passing on this requirement, the state limited its financial responsibility for the demonstration to the federal funds available from JTPA Title III.

Under Title III at the time, federal funds allocated to each state had to be matched on a dollar-for-dollar basis by public or private nonfederal resources (U.S. House of Representatives 1982). This match could be in cash, in kind, or in both forms. Up to half of the amount could be met by UI benefits to program participants. Consequently, the overwhelming majority of participants at all sites were UI claimants. In short, fiscal necessity tended to drive program targeting.

Client Assessment

Client assessment should give participants enough information about their job preferences and skills to enable them to conduct an effective job search and choose among their training opportunities. It should also provide program staff with the information needed to develop individual service plans.

TEC/HCC conducted separate client assessments at three different points in the program. An initial assessment was conducted by Career Circles during the first week of participation. This activity was primarily a self-assessment to help participants examine their personal preferences and skills.[8] TEC counselors then conducted their own assessments during the job-search workshop that followed the Career Circles module. These assessments were based more on personal interviews than on formal instruments. Last, participants who were referred for Tier II classroom training were assessed informally by HCC staff to determine which course offerings, if any, were suitable.

Assessment at SEE began during the first week of the program, when instructors observed all class members during their job-search workshop. Participants also were interviewed by a job developer, who took information on their work histories and educations. A series of tests covering job-skill aptitudes, plus math and basic educational achievement, was then conducted. Test results were interpreted for participants and made available to job developers.

SER/JOBS did not institute formal testing during the demonstration.[9] Instead, job developers gleaned information from their interviews with participants. These interviews provided an initial contact point for staff and participants and helped staff learn about the needs of individual participants. Job developers met daily to discuss the job market and participants' progress.

Tier I: Job-Search Assistance

TEC/HCC Tier I was a six-week program with three distinct segments:

1. A week-long, full-day career exploration module operated by Career Circles
2. A week-long, half-day job-search workshop operated by TEC
3. A four-week job club operated by TEC, with attendance weekly or as needed

The Career Circles module focused on long-range strategic issues. It took participants through a series of introspective paper-and-pencil exercises designed to elicit fundamental aptitudes, desires, and career goals. Career Circles stressed individual work more than group interaction. In addition, perhaps making it unique among publicly-sponsored job-search programs, Career Circles was located in an upscale shopping center in a high-income neighborhood. Its combination of extensive written work, emphasis on individual activities, and upper-middle-class setting was clearly geared toward white-collar professionals.

The second TEC/HCC Tier I segment was a job-search workshop operated by TEC staff who worked exclusively on the demonstration.

This week-long, half-day activity took place in a location set apart from regular TEC offices to avoid potential problems due to commonly-held negative perceptions about *unemployment offices*. The workshop focused on short-range tactical issues of finding a job. Each morning, TEC staff worked with participants on job-finding skills, including how to find and use available information about job openings, write a resume, contact an employer by letter and on the phone, enhance personal grooming, and conduct an effective job interview.

In addition, the workshop's half-day format gave participants an opportunity to put their newly learned job-search skills to immediate use by contacting employers each afternoon. These efforts were reinforced by individual meetings with program staff about issues and problems that arose during the job-search process.

The last segment of TEC/HCC Tier I was a job club, with daily attendance recommended and weekly attendance required. The job club was a less structured experience that enabled participants to use program facilities such as reference materials, a telephone message center, a phone bank, a xerox machine, and typewriters.

Tier I at SEE began with a week-long, half-day job-search workshop. These workshops started with individual assessments, followed by a mix of activities. Next came a job club that met on Wednesday afternoons. Attendance was recommended for current workshop participants and recent workshop graduates. The SEE job club invited local employers to discuss the job market and meet participants. In addition, it provided a forum for SEE job developers to share current leads with participants, thus offering strong incentives for participants to attend.

SER/JOBS Tier I offerings were similar to most job-search programs. This week-long, half-day sequence began with an informal assessment of participants, based on extensive individual interviews. Subsequent activities emphasized finding job openings, writing resumes, and contacting employers. On the last day, participants conducted mock job interviews which were videotaped and critiqued by staff members and other participants. This program element culminated with a graduation ceremony.

SER/JOBS had no required job club *per se*. Instead, its participants had to generate five job contacts and relate their experiences to other job-search workshop members. After the workshop, participants were encouraged to visit program offices—which were open daily—to review job listings on microfiche. In addition, they were urged to contact their assigned counselor/job developer at least twice a week.

Tier II: Retraining

Table 1.4 indicates that Tier II at TEC/HCC focused overwhelmingly on classroom training, Tier II at SER/JOBS focused overwhelmingly on OJT, and Tier II at SEE reflected an even mix of these activities.

Table 1.4
Tier II Activity Mix
(percent)

Activity	TEC/HCC	SEE	SER/JOBS
Classroom training	83	50	13
OJT	17	50	87
Total	100	100	100

TEC/HCC's emphasis on classroom training reflected the fact that one of its co-contractors, Houston Community College, had the lead responsibility for this part of the program. In addition, OJT—traditionally used to provide entry-level jobs—was not appropriate for the experienced white-collar participants at this site. Hence, OJT was used only to supply 23 bus drivers for the local transportation authority.

TEC/HCC classroom training was conducted in the form of traditional fixed-duration courses, timed according to the academic calendar. Initial offerings included classes in air conditioning and refrigeration, computer maintenance technology, and computer-command automotive electronic technology. In response to the mismatch between the mostly white-collar backgrounds of TEC/HCC participants and the blue-collar orientation of its offerings, HCC later added a course on computer-assisted drafting.

SER/JOBS provided classroom training to only 13 percent of its Tier II participants (10 persons). This group was trained to become secretaries and automobile mechanics. Given the site's objective, to place participants in income-generating situations as quickly as possible, OJT was used to the maximum feasible extent. Another factor that prompted use of this option was that OJT wages counted toward the site's resource match. In addition, participants' prior wages were not so high that placement in an OJT slot would produce major wage losses. Given all of these factors, SER/JOBS exhausted its OJT budget and subsequently felt this activity had been underfunded.

As mentioned, SEE provided an even mix of classroom training and OJT, which indicated a flexibility to reach beyond its existing in-house capabilities. Classroom training focused either on adult basic education (preparation for a GED examination and English as a second language) or on basic occupational skills training.[10] Occupational training emphasized typing, bookkeeping, retail sales and medical-ward clerking—traditionally female jobs. These courses were three-week exposures to each occupation, offered on a flexible open-entry, open-exit basis. Their primary goal was to familiarize trainees with an occupation and enable them to be comfortable in an entry-level job interview.

OJT was used by SEE to place participants in a number of different jobs. This option was motivated by many of the same forces discussed above. As was the case for SER/JOBS, the staff at SEE felt that OJT had been underfunded relative to other program activities.

The Project Sponsor and Evaluation Contractor

Many forces shaped the Worker Adjustment Demonstration and determined its success. Foremost among these was the project's sponsor, the Texas Department of Community Affairs.[11] TDCA had the foresight, imagination, commitment, and perseverance to recognize the need for a project of this type and to see it to completion. Not only did TDCA commission a series of demonstration projects, but equally important, it mandated an evaluation and insisted that this evaluation meet the highest possible methodological standards.

This was particularly noteworthy at the time because there was little experience upon which to base plans for JTPA Title III programs, and the federal government was providing limited guidance to the states, who had to implement them.[12] Hence, TDCA was attempting to fill an information void that was national as well as statewide.

The TDCA request for proposals established the generic two-tier model for all sites. It also set forth parameters for targeting clients and providing services. In addition, by passing the JTPA Title III matching requirement through to the demonstration sites, TDCA influenced their client recruitment strategies. It also played a key role during implementation of the project by promoting site cooperation and providing technical assistance to help interpret program requirements and address problems that arose.

Another key force in the development and promotion of the demonstration was the State Job Training Coordinating Council.[13] The SJTCC was particularly influential in creating the demonstration, determining its two-tier generic program model, and selecting local sites.

A third key actor was the evaluation contractor, Abt Associates, Inc. of Cambridge, Massachusetts. Abt Associates was selected by TDCA after the projects were chosen, but before they were implemented. Thus, the evaluation team came in after the fact, but not too late to design an evaluation that could be administered as an integral part of the demonstration.

Efforts by the evaluation team, in concert with those by site personnel and TDCA staff, produced a successful demonstration and evaluation. Random assignment was executed rigorously and its integrity was maintained scrupulously. Data collection was comprehensive, detailed, and minimally disruptive to the sites. Furthermore, evaluation staff maintained a constant presence at each site to ensure that all major issues and activities were dealt with and fully documented.

Local Labor Market Conditions

Labor market conditions were another factor that influenced the final form of the demonstration projects and determined their success.

Economic conditions faced by TEC/HCC in Houston were markedly different from those confronted by SEE and SER/JOBS in El Paso. For example, consider their local populations (table 1.5).

Table 1.5
1980 Population Characteristics

	Houston (Harris County)	El Paso County
Population	2,409,500	479,900
Median family income ($)[a]	20,800	14,000
	(percent)	(percent)
White (non-Hispanic)	63	33
Black (non-Hispanic)	19	4
Hispanic	15	62
High school graduate	70	59
Labor force participant[b]	72	61

SOURCE: 1980 U.S. Census.
a. 1979.
b. Persons 16 and older.

The Houston area (Harris County), with a 1980 population of almost 2.5 million, dwarfed the El Paso area (El Paso County), with less than half a million residents. In addition, the composition of these populations differed markedly. Houston was a large modern city. Its 1980 population was diverse (63 percent white, 19 percent black, and 15 percent Hispanic), well-educated (70 percent high school graduates), active in the labor force (72 percent participants), and relatively high-income ($20,800 per family, annually).

In contrast, El Paso was a predominantly Hispanic border city. Its 1980 population was 62 percent Hispanic and 16 percent of the community did not speak English at home (as opposed to 4 percent in Houston). Correspondingly, El Paso residents were less well-educated (only 59 percent were high school graduates); they were less likely to be labor force members (61 percent participated); and their family incomes were much lower ($14,000 annually).

El Paso's low income reflected not only the more limited education of its residents, but also competition from the virtually inexhaustible supply of low-wage laborers able to commute daily across the river from Mexico. Further compounding this problem was a continuing loss of manufacturing jobs to Mexico.

In terms of aggregate employment distributions by industry and occupation (table 1.6), Houston and El Paso looked somewhat alike. Their most obvious difference was the fact that government employment was far more extensive in El Paso (21 percent of all jobs) than in Houston (11 percent of all jobs).

But these aggregate similarities mask dramatic differences that become clear upon further inspection. For example, Houston wage rates (table 1.7) were far higher than those in El Paso. This was especially true for manufacturing, which paid over twice as much in Houston. In addition, Houston manufacturing jobs paid over 20 percent more than other local jobs, whereas El Paso manufacturing jobs paid somewhat less than other jobs.

Because manufacturing was the primary source of economic displacement in both cities, subsequent wage losses were potentially larger in Houston than in El Paso. Furthermore, it may have been easier to identify key sources of displacement in El Paso and thereby target program resources, because its manufacturing firms were more than twice as large as those in Houston. Hence, displacement in El Paso may have been more concentrated among fewer larger firms. On the other hand, El Paso had a weaker overall economy with much higher unemployment. Thus, its reemployment prospects probably were dimmer.

Figure 1.1 illustrates this situation. During 1980–81, unemployment was about 4 percent in Houston, but over twice that rate in El Paso. For the next two years, unemployment rose sharply in both cities, peaking at over 12 percent in El Paso and 9 percent in Houston. Plans for the Worker Adjustment Demonstration were based on conditions that prevailed during 1983—when unemployment peaked—but the program

Table 1.6
Employment by Industry and Occupation
(percent)

	Houston (Harris County)	El Paso County
Industry		
Services	27	29
Manufacturing	18	19
Retail trade	15	18
Construction	10	6
Finance, insurance, real estate	7	6
Wholesale trade	6	5
Transportation	5	5
Public administration	3	7
Communications, utilities	3	4
Mining	5	0
Agriculture, forestry, fishery	1	1
Occupation		
Administrative support	19	17
Precision products	15	12
Professional	13	12
Sales	11	12
Services	10	13
Executive, administrative, managerial	12	10
Machine operators	6	10
Handlers, helpers	5	5
Transport operators	4	5
Technical	4	3
Farming	1	1
Government workers	11	21

SOURCE: 1980 U.S. Census.

was conducted in 1984, by which time unemployment had dropped to 10 percent in El Paso and 7 percent in Houston. Thus, some plans for the program, especially for client recruitment, had to be changed, and some plans that were not changed resulted in services that did not match prevailing conditions.

Table 1.7
Mean Wages and Firm Size

	Houston (Harris County)	El Paso County
Annualized wages ($)		
All private jobs	22,100	13,900
Manufacturing	26,900	13,600
Workers per employer		
All private jobs	22	18
Manufacturing	44	78

SOURCE: Texas Employment Commission for September 1984.

Table 1.8 provides a different look at the economic condition of the sites by summarizing their employment and unemployment by industry. A comparison of these distributions indicates the extent to which specific industries were under- or over-represented among the unemployed. It should be noted, however, that while the figures in table 1.8 are the best available, they are only rough approximations.

Perhaps most striking is the fact that 36 percent of El Paso's unemployed were from apparel manufacturing, which represented only 10 percent of the county's total employment. This finding is consistent with major reported layoffs in the apparel industry and program staff perceptions that this industry was in a serious decline.

At the opposite extreme, 31 percent of the El Paso jobs, but only 13 percent of its unemployment, came from wholesale and retail trade. Likewise, 21 percent of the jobs, but only 12 percent of the unemploy-

Figure 1.1
Houston and El Paso Unemployment Rates

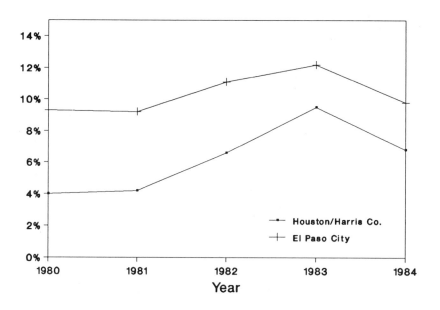

ment, came from service industries in El Paso. Thus, trade and service jobs may have been potential local targets of reemployment opportunity.

Houston experienced a serious—although less concentrated—recession, with fewer pronounced unemployment differences across industries. This more balanced response probably reflected Houston's larger and more diverse economy. The main exception, however, was contract construction, which produced 23 percent of the local unemployment, but comprised only 10 percent of the local jobs, perhaps indicating construction's sensitivity to downturns in other sectors.

Underrepresented among Houston's unemployed, and thereby comprising a potential source of reemployment opportunities, were the trade and service industries. This situation, although not as pronounced as in El Paso, mirrors a national trend toward general expansion of the service sector.

Table 1.8
Percent of Total Employment and Total Unemployment by Industry

Percent by industry	Houston (Harris County)		El Paso County	
	Employed	Unemployed	Employed	Unemployed
Manufacturing				
Apparel	0	0	10	36
Primary, metals, machinery	0	10	2	3
Petroleum	1	1	0	0
Other	12	7	14	14
Contract construction	10	23	7	8
Wholesale, retail trade	29	22	31	13
Services	24	19	21	12
Finance, insurance, real estate	8	6	6	3
Public utility	8	5	7	2
Mining	7	4	0	0
Other, missing	0	3	0	8
Total number	1,229,600	16,800	139,600	4,400

SOURCE: Texas Employment Commission for September 1984. Columns do not sum to 100 percent due to discrepancies in source tables. Unemployment data by industry are approximate.

In summary, then, it appears that:

1. The El Paso economy was considerably weaker, with higher unemployment and lower wage rates
2. Displacement in El Paso was more concentrated in specific industries and larger firms
3. The El Paso labor force was less diverse and had more limited skills, especially with respect to education and English-speaking ability

NOTES

1. A $300,000 project operated by ARMCO Steel and the United Steelworkers of America also was funded, but was not part of the demonstration.

2. The Cameron County project was originally planned as part of the demonstration, but local management problems delayed its implementation for several years.

3. The Emergency Jobs, Training and Family Assistance Act of 1983.

4. Plans for the Worker Adjustment Demonstration were conceived by a small group working out of the governor's office between April and September 1983. The group's original intent was to fund the projects and their evaluation simultaneously. However, a reorganization began in September 1983, which caused funding of the evaluation to be delayed until Phase 2 of the demonstration.

5. Especially important were the severance/retraining package agreed to as part of a Texaco refinery closing in Port Arthur and a large program funded through the governor's Title III discretionary funds.

6. This TEC/HCC design grew out of discussions with the state and the evaluation contractor. Its goal was to compare impacts of Tier I only and Tier I plus Tier II services.

7. JTPA Title III, 1982, section 302 (a) specifies that "Each State is authorized to establish procedures to identify substantial groups of eligible individuals who—

1. have been terminated, laid off, or who have received a notice of termination or layoff from employment, are eligible for or have exhausted their entitlement to unemployment compensation and are unlikely to return to their previous industry or occupation
2. have been terminated or who have received a notice of termination of employment, as a result of any permanent closure of a plant or facility
3. are long-term unemployed and have limited opportunities for employment or reemployment in the same or a similar occupation in the area in which such individuals reside, including any older individuals who may have substantial barriers to employment by reason of age

8. Career Circles used a variety of introspective exercises much like those in the popular job-search manual, *What Color is Your Parachute?* (Bolles 1984).

9. It introduced testing soon thereafter, however.

10. In the study, 66 SEE Tier II sample members participated in 86 classroom training elements; hence, some persons participated in more than one element. Most often, this represented a situation in which basic education was followed by occupational training.

11. The demonstration was sponsored by the Training and Employment Development Division of the Texas Department of Community Affairs. TDCA Assistant Director for Research, Demonstration and Evaluation, Christopher T. King, was the prime mover for the demonstration. When he left TDCA in July 1985, Mary Jane Leheigh, who had been with the project for several years, assumed primary responsibility.

12. The main existing sources of information about displaced worker programs were the Downriver Community Conference Economic Readjustment Program (Kulik, Smith, and Stromsdorfer 1984), the Buffalo Dislocated Worker Demonstration (Corson, Long, and Maynard 1985) and the Delaware Dislocated Worker Program (Bloom 1987a).

13. Individuals who played a particularly important role were Ray Marshall, chair of the state's Job Training Coordinating Council, and Judge Richard LeBlanc, chair of its Worker Adjustment Committee.

2
The Evaluation

This chapter describes the evaluation of the Worker Adjustment Demonstration. Specifically, it introduces the key impact questions addressed, describes the evaluation designs used, and discusses major implementation issues. Appendix 2.1 describes the statistical procedures employed to estimate program impacts.

Impact Questions

Program impacts are the outcomes caused by the program. By definition, they are the difference between treatment group outcomes with the program and what these outcomes would have been without it. For example, if 85 percent of a treatment group became reemployed within six months after a program and 80 percent would have become reemployed without it, the net impact of the program is a 5-percentage point reemployment gain.

The Worker Adjustment Demonstration addressed the following key impact questions:

1. What was the net impact of Tier I job-search assistance?
2. What was the net impact of Tier I/II job-search assistance plus retraining?
3. What was the differential impact of Tier I/II versus Tier I Only?

Each of the preceding impact questions was addressed in terms of three basic outcomes:

1. earnings
2. employment
3. UI benefits

The expressed goal of the demonstration was to expedite reemployment in jobs that minimized wage loss. Achieving this goal would, in turn, increase future earnings and reduce the amount of UI benefits required; hence, the outcome measures used for the impact analysis directly reflect the goals of the program.

Ideally, one should measure program impacts over the remaining working life of participants. In order to be useful, however, an evaluation must provide findings in time to inform policy decisions. To strike a balance between these two competing objectives, a one-year follow-up period was established.

The evaluation estimated impacts separately for men and women. This distinction reflects major differences between the labor market experiences of each and the fact that prior studies have consistently documented larger program impacts for women (Bassi 1984; Bloom 1987b; Bryant and Rupp 1987; Dickinson, Johnson and West 1986; and Kiefer 1979).[1]

The evaluation also examined impacts by site to account for the different program content, target groups, and local economic conditions of each. In addition, it explored how impacts varied by participants' education, occupation, age, prior earnings, duration of prior employment, and duration of unemployment.

Last, the evaluation distinguished between the effects of being offered program services, referred to hereafter as *treatment group impacts,* and the effects of actually receiving services, referred to hereafter as *participant impacts.* This distinction reflects the inevitable fact that not all persons assigned to a program will participate.

Experimental Designs

The evaluation was a randomized experiment, in which eligible applicants were randomly assigned to alternative experimental groups. This lottery approach is widely acknowledged to be the most powerful existing methodology for measuring program impacts (Riecken and Boruch 1974; Hausman and Wise 1985; Stromsdorfer et al. 1985; Betsey, Hollister and Papageorgiou 1985). Randomized experiments attain their methodological power from the laws of probability, which produce treatment and control groups that are initially comparable in all respects; the larger the samples, the greater their probable comparability.

Randomly assigned experimental groups tend to be comparable in terms of measurable characteristics such as age, education, and prior job experience. Moreover, and of greater importance, they are comparable in terms of unmeasured factors such as motivation, intelligence, and emotional stability. Therefore, any subsequent differences between outcomes for these groups can be attributed to differences in the treatments to which they were exposed.

The three-group random assignment model shown in figure 2.1 was implemented by TEC/HCC. This design was judged to be feasible because of the site's successful prior program experience, its willingness to manage a more complex evaluation design, and its large expected client flow. Accordingly, TEC/HCC applicants were recruited and screened at Houston TEC offices. Eligible applicants were listed on a random assignment log, which was collected each week by the evaluation contractor. The evaluation contractor then assigned names on this log to Tier I Only, Tier I/II, or control status using a random number table. Project staff were notified of random assignment results within one day. They subsequently scheduled program enrollment for treatment group members by phone and letter. Control group members were informed of their status by letter.

Table 2.1 lists the types of impact estimates that are possible from the TEC/HCC random assignment model. For example, the net impact of being offered Tier I services can be estimated by comparing the post-random assignment experiences of Tier I Only treatment group members and controls. Similarly, the net impact of being offered a Tier I/II sequence can be estimated by comparing Tier I/II and control group experiences. Tier I/II versus Tier I differential impacts can be estimated by comparing net impacts for these two treatment streams.[2]

SEE and SER/JOBS implemented the two-group random assignment model shown in figure 2.2. This simpler design reflected their smaller expected client flow and the newness of their programs. The first step in the process was a referral, a walk-in, or plant-based recruitment of a program applicant. The next step was eligibility determination by local project staff. Eligible applicants then were listed on a random assignment log that was submitted weekly to the evaluation contractor.

Figure 2.1
The TEC/HCC Random Assignment Model

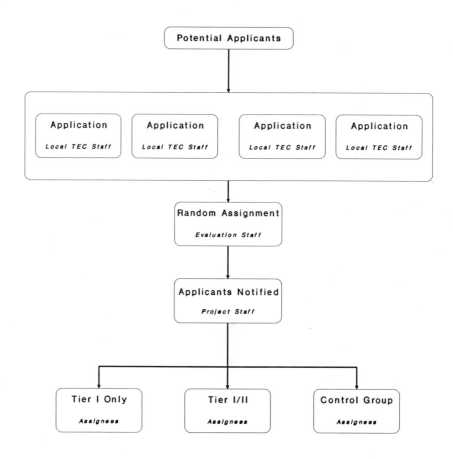

Table 2.1
Impact Estimates from Each Random Assignment Model

	TEC/HCC	SEE	SER/JOBS
Tier I net impact	Yes		
Tier I/II net impact	Yes	Yes	Yes
Tier I/II vs. Tier I differential impact	Yes		

The evaluation contractor randomly assigned names on the log to a Tier I/II treatment group or control status. Program staff were informed of these assignments and, in turn, informed treatment and control group members. Comparison of subsequent Tier I/II and control group outcomes produced net impact estimates for the Tier I/II sequence of program activities.

Implementation

Implementing the evaluation required careful planning, extensive negotiation, continual support from the project sponsor, active cooperation from site staff, vigilant monitoring by the evaluation team, and considerable luck. The first step in the process was to reach agreement with TDCA on the basic evaluation approach. This was facilitated by the fact that the TDCA assistant director who initiated the demonstration had over a decade of experience in employment and training research.[3] Hence, both he and his staff were well aware of the substantive and methodological issues involved.

Of particular importance to the choice of a randomized experimental design was the growing disenchantment by researchers with existing nonexperimental alternatives. Although not published until much later, analyses of the major problems with nonexperimental methods used to evaluate CETA were being circulated at the time (Fraker and Maynard 1987; LaLonde 1986; LaLonde and Maynard 1987).

Figure 2.2
The SEE and SER/JOBS Random Assignment Model

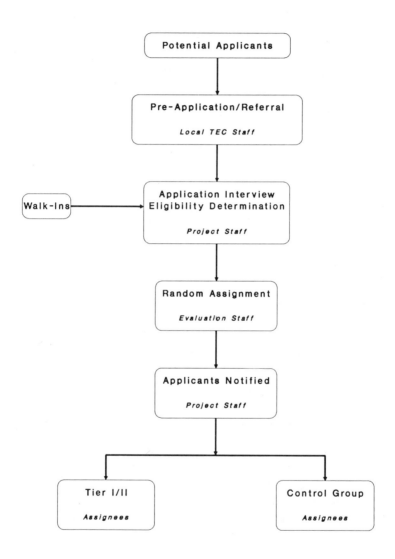

In addition, two prestigious national advisory committees were studying the problems of nonexperimental employment and training program evaluations. Both committees subsequently published reports that strongly recommended randomized experimental designs (Betsey, Hollister and Papageorgiou 1985; Stromsdorfer et al. 1985).

Furthermore, JTPA Title III was a new national program; hence, the evaluation had a national *and* a statewide audience. This produced additional pressure for meeting the highest methodological standards possible. Although TDCA staff who created the demonstration were well aware of these issues, they had to convince many others of their importance before a randomized experiment was accepted by the agency.

Having done so, the next step was to work with each site to develop a suitable plan. Because the evaluation contractor was selected after the Phase 2 demonstration projects had been chosen, the evaluation was not developed in conjunction with initial local plans. Nevertheless, each project was selected on the condition that it be part of an evaluation. Thus, site personnel knew they would have evaluation responsibilities, but they did not know what these responsibilities would be.

It was first necessary to convince sites that a rigorous evaluation was essential. The most compelling argument toward this end was the widely acknowledged fact that employment and training programs had almost no sound evaluation support. This lack of support was especially problematic given the attacks being launched against employment and training programs and budgetary pressures on all social programs during the early Reagan years.

Having established the importance of a rigorous evaluation, it then was necessary to address the issue of *why* random assignment should be used. Here the growing acknowledgement by employment and training researchers of the weaknesses of nonexperimental evaluation methods was most telling.

The two greatest obstacles to getting and maintaining local staff cooperation, however, were site concerns about:

1. the requirement that program services be withheld from controls
2. the requirement that program services be offered to all treatment group members

Not serving controls produced two related concerns. The first was *denial of services*. Program staff cared deeply about helping persons in need; thus the idea of withholding services for any reason was difficult to accept.

With scarce resources, however, not all eligible persons can be served by a program. In this context, allocating limited program slots by a lottery, with an equal chance for every applicant to be chosen, is ethically defendable. Furthermore, it is fairer than the idiosyncratic selection procedures often used by local programs. Site staff acknowledged this argument, but denial of service to controls remained a lingering source of discomfort for them.

A related concern involved the additional recruitment necessary to generate a control group. Although many more persons were eligible for the demonstration than could be served, sites worried about their ability to recruit enough applicants. Hence, from the outset, TDCA committed its resources to assist sites with recruitment, if necessary.

In addition to their reservations about not serving controls, site staff were worried about offering program services to all treatment group members (*serving all comers*). This reflected their concern about not meeting performance expectations and thereby losing potential future funding. Staff expected some members of the treatment group to be different from the types of clients they were equipped to serve. Such persons normally would be given low priority. Now they would have to be served. Doing so might reduce measured performance in terms of traditional indicators such as placement rates and average cost per placement.

TDCA therefore allowed each site to set its own performance goals instead of establishing formal performance standards.[4] TDCA also agreed that because of unique demonstration demands, no sanctions would be applied if a site failed to meet its goals. Although doing so was necessary and sufficient to gain site cooperation, local staff were never fully comfortable with this issue.

The next step in implementing the evaluation was to create a management process that would ensure its methodological integrity. Specifically, it was necessary—

1. to ensure that program services were allocated only by random assignment

2. to minimize the number of control group members who received program services (*crossovers*)
3. to minimize the number of treatment group members who did not receive program services (*no-shows*)
4. to ensure adequate sample build-up

To help ensure that all experimental assignments were random, this process was conducted solely by the evaluation contractor. Moreover, it was conducted off site premises and based only on random numbers.

To minimize crossovers, the evaluation contractor checked every random assignment log against the control group roster. In addition, sites were not given credit toward their performance goals for serving controls. Furthermore, the evaluation contractor monitored local program records to check for control group members who were enrolled by mistake. Ultimately, there were only 20 crossovers out of 784 control group members (less than 3 percent).

Even given the preceding precautions, however, the potential for undocumented services to controls remained. As a further preventive measure, sites were warned that serving controls would weaken their measured program impacts by improving control group outcomes. In addition, sites were allowed to refer controls to other local organizations, which relieved some of the pressure to serve them. Hence, estimates of Worker Adjustment Demonstration impacts reflect the program's effect relative to services that probably would have been received in its absence. Because Houston and El Paso employment and training services for displaced workers were quite limited, the control group alternatives represent *weak treatments*, comprising mostly counseling and access to job listings from the state Employment Service.

No-shows (treatment group members who did not receive services) were a third key implementation issue. This phenomenon reflected applicants' decisions not to proceed (because they had found a job, they did not have sufficient motivation, or they did not expect the benefits of participation to be sufficient) and site staff decisions not to serve specific applicants (because of their ineligibility, personal idiosyncrasies, or lack of appropriate services).

No-shows reduce one's ability to detect program impacts, because they dilute the contrast between services received by treatment and control group members. The greater the proportion of treatment group members who become no-shows, the smaller the actual difference between services received by treatment and control group members.

One approach used to reduce this problem was to conduct random assignment as late as possible in the client intake process. This implied that more motivational hurdles would come before random assignment and thereby screen out persons who were least able or willing to participate. Hence, much of the natural drop-off between a first inquiry and participation occurred *before* random assignment.

However, the methodological rationale for delaying random assignment conflicted with local staff desires to minimize their contact with applicants who subsequently became control group members. Hence, sites wanted to place random assignment as early as possible during intake. The random assignment models described above reflect a compromise between these competing objectives.

A second approach used to minimize no-shows was to reduce the time between program application and notification about the outcome of random assignment. From this perspective, it would have been ideal to inform applicants immediately, as they waited in a program office. This was not feasible, however, due to logistical and budgetary constraints. Thus, a compromise was agreed upon whereby sites submitted eligible applications weekly, evaluation staff informed sites of random assignment results within a day, and applicants were informed by sites immediately thereafter.

A third approach used to reduce no-shows called for sites to contact treatment group members who missed their scheduled appointments and aggressively promote participation. This was done most extensively by SER/JOBS, which consequently experienced only a 13-percent no-show rate.

A fourth major implementation problem was maintaining adequate sample build-up. Inadequate sample size can reduce the statistical precision of program impact estimates and thereby threaten the usefulness of an evaluation. As mentioned earlier, this issue soon became acute at SEE and SER/JOBS. In response, TDCA arranged for the El Paso TEC branch to refer UI claimants; thereafter, sample build-up was no longer a problem. All sites met or exceeded their sample goals (table 2.2), producing a total sample of 2,259 persons.

Table 2.2
Planned Versus Actual Sample Size

	Planned sample	Actual sample	Planned Tier II	Actual Tier II
TEC/HCC				
Tier I only	250	332	0	0
Tier I/II	350	467	200	132
Control	250	255		
SEE				
Tier I/II	250	299	125	119
Control	250	243		
SER/JOBS				
Tier I/II	250	347	125	77
Control	250	316		
Total/overall	1,850	2,259	450	328

Estimating Program Impacts

Because random assignment in large samples produces comparable treatment and control groups, valid net program impact estimates can be derived from a simple comparison of treatment and control group mean outcomes. The statistical precision of this analysis can be improved, however, by using multiple regression to control for differences in observed individual characteristics. Doing so reduces the amount of *noise* (unexplained variation) in the analysis and thereby increases its resolution; hence, using multiple regression is equivalent to increasing effective sample size.

The multiple regression model used to estimate treatment group impacts (the effect of being offered program services) is described in appendix 2.1. A further analytic step, also described in appendix 2.1, was required to convert treatment group impacts into impacts per participant (the effect of actually receiving services).

NOTES

1. Most prior studies of employment and training programs have focused on economically disadvantaged persons who had never held *good jobs*. Hence, their observed difference between impacts for men and women may not apply to displaced workers. Nevertheless, because the labor market experiences of men and women differ so much in all industries and occupations, it seemed appropriate to estimate their program impacts separately.

2. An equivalent way to estimate differential Tier I versus Tier I/II impacts is to compare their post-assignment outcomes directly.

3. The TDCA Division of Training and Employment Development sponsored the demonstration. TDCA Assistant Director for Research, Demonstration and Evaluation, Christopher T. King, was the lead person for the project. Dr. King is currently Senior Research Associate at the Center for the Study of Human Resources, Lyndon B. Johnson School of Public Affairs, University of Texas at Austin.

4. At the time, JTPA Title II-A was implementing a formal performance-based management system, whereby each state was to judge the performance of its local Service Delivery Areas (SDAs) against explicit standards set in accord with their client mix and economic conditions. This system, which is still a key feature of Title II-A and Title III, was a major issue, and program staff were especially sensitive to anything that might affect their measured performance, regardless of whether or not formal standards existed.

Appendix 2.1
Program Impact Estimation Procedure

Site-specific treatment group impacts (the effects of being offered demonstration program services) were estimated from multiple regression models of the following form:[1]

$$Y_i = a + \sum_j B_j \cdot X_{ji} + \sum_k C_k \cdot SITE_{ki} + \sum_m D_m \cdot GROUP_{mi} + e_i \qquad [A1]$$

where:

Y_i = earnings, employment, or UI benefits for person i;

X_{ji} = characteristic j (race, education, age, prior occupation, random assignment week, and in some models, prior earnings, employment, or UI benefits) for person i;

$SITE_{ki}$ = (1/0) dummy variables SEE and SER/JOBS, to indicate the site for person i (TEC/HCC was the implicit baseline);

$GROUP_{mi}$ = (1/0) dummy variables TEC/HCC1, TEC/HCC12, SEE12 and SER/JOBS12, to indicate the treatment group for person i (site-specific control status was the implicit baseline);

e_i = a random error term;

B_j = regression coefficients for individual characteristics;

C_k = site differences in underlying control group outcomes;

D_m = the net impact for treatment group m relative to its site-specific control group; and

a = the intercept.

Equation A1 was estimated for the full sample of men and the El Paso sample of women, separately for each outcome variable. By controlling statistically for individual characteristics, it was possible to *net out* their effects. For example, controlling for education eliminated this source of earnings variation among sample members. Likewise, controlling for demonstration site eliminated that portion of earnings variation due to site-specific factors.

Treatment group impact estimates were obtained from the coefficients, D_m, for the treatment group variables. These coefficients represent differences between mean outcomes for a specific treatment group and its control group counterpart, controlling for individual characteristics in the model.

Ordinary least squares regressions were used to estimate impacts on continuous outcome measures such as earnings and UI benefits received. Maximum likelihood LOGIT models were used to estimate program impacts on discrete outcome measures such as employment and UI benefit receipt rates. Appropriate steps were taken to convert LOGIT-based impact estimates into

39

percentage terms. This was accomplished by converting impacts on log-odds (the LOGIT coefficients) to impacts on probabilities (Pindyck and Rubinfeld 1976), and expressing the resulting probabilities in percentage terms.[2]

The preceding regression-adjusted treatment and control outcome differences measured the effects of being *offered* program services, not the effect of actually *receiving* them. To estimate this latter effect required further analytic steps. To understand their rationale consider how the average treatment group impact (the difference between treatment and control group outcomes) is related to the average impact per participant and the impact per no-show (approximately zero). Equation A2 summarizes this relationship.

$$E(\bar{Y}_T) - E(\bar{Y}_C) = r \cdot 0 + (1 - r) \, PI \qquad [A2]$$

where:

$E(\bar{Y}_T) =$ the expected mean treatment group outcome;
$E(\bar{Y}_C) =$ the expected mean control group outcome;
$r =$ the proportion of the treatment group that did not participate (the no-show rate);
$PI =$ the true impact for participants; and
$0 =$ the approximate impact for no-shows.

Substituting the observed treatment and control group mean outcomes, $\bar{Y}_T$ and $\bar{Y}_C$, for their expected values yields a statistically consistent estimator of impacts per participant (Bloom 1984a).

$$\hat{PI} = \frac{\bar{Y}_T - \bar{Y}_C}{(1 - r)} \qquad [A3]$$

Hence, to estimate program impacts per participant, one can simply compute the treatment and control group outcome difference and divide by one minus the proportional no-show rate. This procedure also applies to *regression-adjusted* differences in means (Bloom 1984a).

Consider the following example. If annual treatment group post-assignment earnings averaged $6,000, control group earnings averaged $5,500, and 20 percent or 0.2 of the treatment group were no-shows, then the estimated impact per participant would be:

$$\hat{PI} = \frac{\$6,000 - \$5,500}{(1 - 0.2)}$$

$$= \frac{\$500}{0.8}$$

$$= \$625$$

The estimated standard error for this estimator can be approximated as follows (Bloom 1984a):

$$SE(\hat{PI}) = \frac{VAR(\bar{Y}_T) - VAR(\bar{Y}_C)}{(1 - r)} \qquad [A4]$$

To use this procedure for discrete outcome variables (employed or not, receiving UI or not) one must substitute treatment and control outcome proportions for their corresponding outcome means.[3]

Two conditions are necessary for the preceding no-show adjustment to be feasible and valid.

1. Comparable outcome data must be available for participants, no-shows, and controls.
2. No-shows must experience no (or negligible) program impacts.

Without follow-up data for participants and no-shows (the treatment group), and follow-up data for controls, it is not possible to estimate average impacts per treatment group member, which is the starting point for the estimation procedure. Hence, the Worker Adjustment Demonstration data collection plan (chapter 3) was designed to yield follow-up information for all sample members.

If program effects for no-shows differ appreciably from zero, the no-show adjustment will be incorrect. If, for example, no-shows experience large positive impacts, the no-show adjustment will overstate participant impacts. If, on the other hand, no-shows experience large negative impacts, the no-show adjustment will understate participant impacts.

To reduce this risk, no-shows were defined as treatment group members who spent no time in a major program activity. Given the serious labor market problems experienced by sample members, and the weak effects observed for past employment and training programs (Kiefer 1979; Bassi 1984; and Bloom 1987b), such limited program exposure (mostly assessment during intake) was extremely unlikely to affect no-shows appreciably.

As a final note, it is important to recognize that participant impact estimates for the Worker Adjustment Demonstration are only valid for the types of individuals who actually participated.[4] They do not necessarily reflect impacts that would occur if no-shows had participated. Nevertheless, they are the most relevant participant-based impacts to determine because they focus on what happened to the types of persons who actually received demonstration services.

NOTES

1. Pooled impact estimates for all men and for El Paso women were estimated by replacing the site-specific treatment group indicators, $GROUP_{mi}$, with a single treatment group indicator (see table 7.1).

2. The overall site-specific proportion for the dependent variable was used to convert LOGIT coefficients in log-odds to impact estimates in percent. This was accomplished by multiplying the LOGIT coefficient for a specific treatment group impact, times its corresponding site-specific proportion, times one minus this proportion. To convert to percent, this result was multiplied by 100.

3. The no-show adjustment also applies to LOGIT-based estimates of differences in outcome proportions or percentages.

4. These estimates are internally valid, i.e., they are valid for the specific sample and situation that was observed (Campbell 1975).

3
The Data

This chapter describes the data used to evaluate the Worker Adjustment Demonstration. Specifically, it summarizes the information required, outlines the data collection strategy adopted, introduces each major type of data used, and identifies key data sources. Appendices 3.1 and 3.2 examine the validity of outcome data used to measure program impacts.

Data Requirements and Strategy

The Worker Adjustment Demonstration analysis required accurate data on the following:

1. sample characteristics
2. program participation
3. program outcomes
4. program costs
5. program implementation
6. program context

Table 3.1 summarizes how these data were used.

Sample characteristics (age, sex, race, education, and prior occupation) were used for three main purposes. First, they helped define subgroups for separate impact estimates (men versus women; high school graduates versus dropouts; blue-collar versus white-collar workers, etc.). Second, they served as statistical control variables in regression models to increase the precision of program impact estimates. Third, they were used to describe the sample in order to help provide a perspective for generalizing findings.

Table 3.1
Data Requirements

Data	Analytic purpose
Sample characteristics	• Define sample subgroups for impact analysis • Provide control variables to improve precision of impact estimates • Describe sample for generalizing impact findings
Program participation	• Enable no-show corrections for impact estimates • Study the no-show, dropout, and service-receipt selection process • Help interpret impact estimates by describing the treatment received
Program outcomes	• Provide follow-up outcome measures for impact estimates • Provide baseline outcome measures as control variables to improve the precision of impact estimates
Program costs	• Determine the cost-effectiveness of the program at each site • Determine the cost-effectiveness of Tier I vs. Tier I/II programs
Program implementation	• Help interpret impact estimates by delving into the program black box • Provide implementation lessons for future programs
Program context	• Provide an historic, institutional, social, and economic context for interpreting impact findings

Data on program participation and services received by treatment group members were used for three main purposes. First, they provided a basis for computing no-show rates, which were used to estimate impacts per participant (see appendix 2.1). Second, they facilitated analysis of the selection process, which determined who among treatment group members participated, who among participants received Tier II services, and who among Tier II recipients entered classroom training versus OJT. Third, these data provided a context for interpreting impact findings by documenting the mix of services received.

Data on program outcomes (treatment and control group earnings, employment, and UI benefits) were used in two ways. Post-assignment outcomes provided the basis for impact measures. Pre-assignment outcomes were used as control variables in regression models to increase the precision of impact estimates. These measures are the most effective control variables available because they reflect all personal characteristics that influence labor market success (e.g., intelligence, motivation, emotional stability).

Program cost data were used in conjunction with program impact estimates to examine the cost-effectiveness of services provided by the demonstration. These measures were employed to compare the efficiency of programs at the three different sites. In addition, they were used to compare the efficiency of Tier I job-search assistance versus Tier I/II job-search assistance plus occupational skills training.

Information about how the program was implemented helped explain why impacts were or were not observed for particular groups. This information delved into the *black box* of each program and portrayed what actually happened. In addition, the knowledge gained from identifying specific problems that arose, how they were dealt with, and how they might have been avoided, provided valuable insights for the design and management of future displaced worker programs.

Last, information on the historic, institutional, social, and economic background of each project was used to describe its context. This helped to explain why programs developed and performed as they did, which, in turn, produced a richer framework for interpreting and generalizing evaluation findings.

Data Sources

The data collection strategy for the Worker Adjustment Demonstration was designed to:

1. collect only data central to the analysis
2. obtain the highest quality data possible

3. use existing data wherever feasible
4. provide contingency plans

Table 3.2 lists the data sources used, and the following sections describe how each type of data was obtained.

Table 3.2
Data Sources

Data	Sources
Sample characteristics	• JTPA applications • Application addenda
Program participation	• JTPA activity forms • JSA attendance logs
Program outcomes	• UI quarterly wage records • UI weekly benefit records • One-year follow-up survey
Program costs	• Monthly site financial reports
Program implementation	• On-site analyst reports • Key-respondent interviews
Program context	• TEC reports • TDCA reports • SDA reports • U.S. Bureau of Labor Statistics reports • U.S. Census data • Project grant proposals • Local media accounts

Sample Characteristics

Background characteristics for individual sample members were obtained during the application process at each site from information on two forms:

1. a JTPA application form
2. an application addendum

The JTPA application form was part of a uniform statewide JTPA management information system intended for use by TDCA to monitor all of its JTPA programs. The Title III demonstration sites were required to be part of this system, which involved three separate documents: an application form, a program activity form and a 13-week post-program follow-up form. These forms were to be completed by each site and transmitted by computer to TDCA in Austin.

A completed application form was required before an individual could be randomly assigned. This document provided information that identified applicants and described their personal characteristics, military history, prior education, UI benefit history, employment history, family status, and prior JTPA participation, if any. The form was completed by applicants with the help of local staff, where necessary.

Two parallel plans for obtaining these data were developed. The preferred option was to access the statewide TDCA computer file and extract individual records for the demonstration sites. The contingency plan was for sites to duplicate the original copy of each application and provide it to the evaluation contractor for key entry into the project data base.

At the time of the demonstration, the statewide JTPA management information system was undergoing revision. Forms were being changed and a new computer system was being installed to enable direct on-line access for TDCA and every Texas JTPA Service Delivery Area. Each Title III demonstration site was supposed to input forms through its SDA computer. Not unexpectedly, the computer system experienced many start-up problems, and data consequently were obtained from photocopies of completed application forms.

Although the JTPA application form provided the individual background information necessary for analysis, it did not contain sufficient identifying information to locate applicants for the follow-up survey conducted one year after random assignment (discussed below). To provide this tracking information, the evaluation contractor developed a brief application addendum. This form recorded applicants' names, Social Security numbers, and site. In addition, it asked applicants to list the name, address, and telephone number of the ''one person most likely to know where you are" plus "one other person, a friend or relative, with whom you are in touch most frequently."

Participation and Services Received

Two data sources were used to determine who participated in the demonstration program and what services they received. The primary source was the JTPA activity status form, submitted as part of the TDCA information system. This document—the ACCTPAK—was completed for each change in program status experienced by an individual. Thus an ACCTPAK was completed at enrollment to and termination from JTPA. In addition, it was completed at entrance to and completion of specific program activities. Each site provided photocopies of all ACC-TPAKs to the evaluation contractor, who entered the information into the project database.

ACCTPAK data used for the analysis identified: (1) enrollment or not in JTPA (to distinguish no-shows from participants); (2) enrollment or not in OJT or classroom training (to identify sample members who entered Tier II); (3) program enrollment and termination dates (to compute duration of time enrolled); and (4) wage rates and occupations of termination jobs (to gauge the labor market displacement sample experienced by members).

In addition to this information, the evaluation contractor monitored sample members' daily attendance in their first week of Tier I activities. Attendance was recorded on a JSA Attendance Log collected regularly from each site by on-site analysts hired by the evaluation contractor.

Program Outcomes

Outcome data on sample members' earnings, employment, and UI benefits were obtained from local administrative records, supplemented by a brief follow-up survey. Administrative data were obtained from computerized records maintained by the Texas Employment Commission for all workers covered by Unemployment Insurance. This information covered well over 90 percent of all legal jobs in Texas.[1]

Each calendar quarter all *covered* employers must report total wages paid to every employee. This information is retained for five consecutive quarters in individual wage records. As new information is received, data for the least recent quarter are deleted.

By making multiple requests timed appropriately, it was possible to develop individual quarterly earnings histories that included three quarters before random assignment, the quarter in which random assignment occurred, and four quarters after random assignment. Corresponding employment histories were constructed by recording sample members as not employed during quarters with zero UI-covered earnings, and as employed during quarters with non-zero reported earnings. From a separate state computerized record of all UI benefits paid, weekly individual UI benefit histories were constructed for the first 30 weeks after random assignment.

When the project began, it was unclear whether UI wage and benefit records would be available for the time period needed and within the time frame required; thus, contingency plans for a follow-up survey were developed. Subsequently, however, after UI test files were processed successfully, the follow-up survey was scaled back accordingly.

The follow-up survey was conducted one year after random assignment for each sample member. It was administered by telephone with field follow-up, where necessary, by a subcontractor from El Paso.[2] Interviews were conducted in English and Spanish, and took roughly five minutes to complete. Up to eight interview attempts were made during a three-week *window* for each sample member.

Table 3.3 illustrates the success of this effort. The overall response rate was 74 percent, which compares favorably to previous research, especially given the socioeconomic composition of the El Paso subsample. This success was due largely to the vigorous follow-up effort by the survey subcontractor and the high quality of contact information obtained from the application addendum.

Response rates were uniformly high across sites, across treatment groups, and for men and women (table 3.4). In addition, rates were high for both treatment and control groups; hence, initial concerns about control group members refusing to cooperate with follow-up data collection proved to be unfounded. As can be seen, nonresponse was due mostly to problems encountered locating sample members (see table 3.3). Additional nonresponse was encountered because some sample

Table 3.3
Follow-Up Survey Field Experience

| | | Percent of cases | | | |
	Completed	Refused	Located but not contacted	Not located	Total
TEC/HCC I					
I/II	75	3	7	15	100
Control	75	4	5	16	100
	72	5	6	17	100
SEE I/II	70	<1	9	20	100
Control	72	0	4	24	100
SER/JOBS I/II	79	<1	5	16	100
Control	78	0	6	16	100

members who were located were never contacted. For the sample as a whole, only 43 interviews (less than 2 percent) were lost due to refusals.[3]

Table 3.4
Follow-Up Survey Response Rates
(Percent)

		Men	Women
TEC/HCC	I	76	78
	I/II	74	75
	Control	73	74
SEE	I/II	69	70
	Control	69	74
SER/JOBS	I/II	79	80
	Control	76	83

As indicated earlier, the follow-up survey was designed to supplement UI data by providing different measures of reemployment success. One set of survey questions focused on earnings and employment during the interview week, one year after random assignment. These questions provided outcome measures for the longest possible follow-up period. A second set of questions focused on the number of weeks worked during the two quarters prior to the interview. These questions provided employment measures for the third and fourth quarters after random assignment, which roughly approximated the post-program portion of the follow-up period.

Program Costs

Program cost data were obtained from invoices submitted monthly by each site to TDCA. These invoices reported total monthly expenses and separated them into administrative costs, participant support payments, and training-related expenditures. Total cumulative program costs for each site were obtained from this source and provided the basis for cost-effectiveness measures. More extensive data collection required for a comprehensive benefit-cost analysis was beyond the scope of project resources.

Program Implementation

Information about the planning, design, development, and operation of each site was obtained from a local key respondent network and on-site analysts. The key respondent network provided an insider's view of critical issues that arose during the demonstration. Respondents were chosen for their knowledge about the program and related local issues. This group included the local project director, TDCA field representatives, the TEC local office director, union representatives, the JTPA Private Industry Council chair, and other active community representatives.

Information was gathered from key respondents through informal telephone conversations with a senior evaluation staff member who worked from a field office in Houston, which was open throughout the project. Prior to each conversation, key respondents were sent an outline of the issues to be discussed.

On-site analysts were the *eyes and ears* of the evaluation team. They observed program operations, spoke regularly with program staff, and were a central link in the collection of site data. Logs were developed to help on-site analysts study specific issues. These logs formed the basis for monthly written reports documenting issues and problems that arose.

In addition to their research, monitoring, and interviewing roles, on-site analysts were responsible for overseeing accuracy and completion of application forms, governing timing and receipt of program activity forms, providing feedback to sites about random assignment, and monitoring no-show and crossover rates. On-site analysts also collected aggregate project reports on enrollments, terminations, and participation.

Program Context

The final group of data sources used for the evaluation provided information on the economic, social, political, and institutional background of each site. These sources included economic reports by TDCA, TEC, the Bureau of Labor Statistics, local Service Delivery Areas, and the U.S. Census; grant proposals for each program; and local media reports.

NOTES

1. Myers (1989) indicates that 98 percent of the nonagricultural jobs in Texas were covered by Unemployment Insurance in 1986.

2. K Associates was the survey subcontractor.

3. Many surveys of low-income populations have found that inability to locate respondents is more of a problem than outright refusals (e.g., Homans 1972; National Opinion Research Corporation 1987; Jastrzab 1988; Abt Associates Inc. and National Opinion Research Corporation 1990).

Appendix 3.1
Analytic Implications of Follow-Up Survey Nonresponse

Issues

Follow-up surveys were obtained for 74 percent of the experimental sample. Table 3.4 indicates that this high response rate was achieved for men and women, and for treatment and control groups from all three sites. Nevertheless, it is still important to consider how, if at all, survey nonresponse affected treatment and control group outcome comparisons that were the basis for program impact estimates. Consider the three possible treatment and control group survey nonresponse patterns:

1. Random nonresponse
2. Uniform nonresponse
3. Differential nonresponse

Random nonresponse implies no difference between the *expected* (long-run average) characteristics of survey respondents and nonrespondents. Hence, random nonresponse will not distort treatment and control group outcome comparisons in large samples and thus will not bias impact estimates. It will, however, reduce sample size and thereby decrease statistical precision.

Uniform treatment and control group nonresponse changes expected treatment and control group characteristics in the same way. For example, assume that less-educated, lower-income treatment and control group members have lower-than-average response rates. This will increase the average education and income level for the follow-up survey sample. If this increase is the same for treatment and control groups, however, it will not affect their comparability. Consequently, uniform nonresponse will not affect the internal validity of impact estimates. These estimates are valid for the sample observed. Uniform nonresponse will, however, reduce sample size and thereby decrease statistical precision. In addition, it may affect the external validity or generalizability of impact findings by changing the composition of the analysis sample.

Differential nonresponse affects expected treatment and control group characteristics differently; hence, it undermines the internal validity, the external validity, and the statistical precision of program impact estimates. This problem depends on the following factors:

1. The nonresponse rate
2. The amount by which respondents differ from nonrespondents in ways related to outcomes of interest (earnings, employment and UI benefits)
3. The proportion of this difference controlled for by statistical models used to estimate impacts

For example, assume that lower income and education reduce response rates more for controls than for treatment group members. This might occur if treatment group members felt a greater obligation to respond. The treatment group survey sample then would have a lower prior income and education than the control group survey sample. This, in turn, would cause survey-based treatment and control group outcome comparisons to understate program impacts on earnings and employment. To the extent that regression-based impact estimates did not control for this phenomenon, a downward bias would exist.

Respondent Versus Nonrespondent Characteristics

To determine which of the above nonresponse patterns actually occurred and therefore how, if at all, survey-based impact findings might be biased, treatment and control respondents and nonrespondents were compared using follow-up and background data available for both. Follow-up comparisons were based on total UI-reported earnings during the year after random assignment, and total UI benefits during the first 30 weeks after random assignment. Background comparisons were based on age, ethnicity, education, prior occupation, UI status, and the presence of dependents under 18 years of age. Data for these characteristics were obtained from demonstration application forms.[1]

To compare respondents and nonrespondents, it was necessary to control for differences in their distributions across sites, because survey response rates varied somewhat by site. To do so, the average difference between respondent and nonrespondent characteristics was estimated from the following regression.

$$Y_i = a + B_1 \cdot RESPOND_i + B_2 \cdot SEE_i + B_3 \cdot SER/JOBS_i + e_i$$

where:

Y_i = the comparison characteristic for person i;
$RESPOND_i$ = one for survey respondents and zero otherwise;
SEE_i = one for sample members from SEE and zero otherwise;
$SER/JOBS_i$ = one for sample members from SER/JOBS and zero otherwise;
e_i = a random disturbance term;
a = an intercept.

This regression was estimated separately for treatment and control group members. Its coefficient, B_1, represents the average respondent versus nonrespondent difference in the characteristic, Y_i, controlling for response distributions across sites.

Table 3A1.1 summarizes findings for men from all sites, and table 3A1.2 summarizes findings for women from El Paso. Results for Houston women were not reported because their treatment and control groups were not comparable and thus were not included in the program impact analysis (see chapter 4).

Table 3A1.1
Difference Between Characteristics of Survey Respondents
and Nonrespondents, Controlling for Site
(All Men)

	Treatment group	Control group
Follow-up outcomes ($)		
Annual UI earnings	1,444	2,007**
30-week UI benefits	305**	57
Background factors (%)		
Age <35	–11**	5
Age 55+	2	<1
White (non-Hispanic)	3	<1
Black (non-Hispanic)	–4	–3
Hispanic	<1	<1
School dropout	–2	–7
Post-high school	3	–1
White-collar	3	<1
Blue-collar	–2	–4
Receiving UI	<1	3
UI exhaustee	<1	–4
Dependents <18	8*	5

* or ** = a respondent versus nonrespondent difference that is statistically significant at the 0.05 or 0.01 level, two-tail.

First consider the results for men in table 3A1.1. Note that both treatment and control group survey respondents had higher earnings than their nonrespondent counterparts. This is consistent with a general tendency for higher income persons to respond to surveys; however, control group respondents exhibited a somewhat larger earnings advantage over nonrespondents. Hence, the control group survey sample may reflect higher initial earnings power. This, in turn, might cause survey-based findings to understate program-induced earnings gains for men.

Table 3A1.2
Difference Between Characteristics of Survey Respondents
and Nonrespondents, Controlling for Site
(El Paso Women)

	Treatment group	Control group
Follow-up outcomes ($)		
Annual UI earnings	−95	785
30-week UI benefits	−26	−120
Background factors (%)		
Age <35	<1	<1
Age 55+	4	<1
White (non-Hispanic)	2	−6
Black (non-Hispanic)	−4	−2
Hispanic	<1	7**
School dropout	−7	4
Post-high school	3	−9*
White-collar	9**	−12**
Blue-collar	−11**	9*
Receiving UI	4	−1
UI exhaustee	−4	−2
Dependents <18	5	3

* or ** =a respondent versus nonrespondent difference that is statistically significant at the 0.05 or 0.01 level, two-tail.

UI benefit findings support this interpretation. Both treatment and control group respondents received *more* UI benefits during the 30-week follow-up period than their nonrespondent counterparts, but this difference was greater for treatment group members.[2] Hence, the treatment group survey sample for men was more likely to receive UI benefits than the control sample, which, in turn, suggests it may have had weaker labor market prospects.

There was less difference between survey respondent and nonrespondent background characteristics, and less *difference in this difference* between treatment and control group members. The most striking finding was in terms of age: male treatment group respondents were noticeably older than male control group respondents.

Now consider the findings for El Paso women (table 3A1.2). Note that treatment group respondents earned slightly less than nonrespondents; whereas control group respondents earned considerably more than their nonrespondent counterparts. This suggests that the treatment group survey sample had weaker labor market prospects than its control group counterpart; hence, survey results may understate program impacts for El Paso women. UI benefit findings were consistent with this interpretation.

Last, note that within the El Paso female survey sample, controls had a greater proportion of Hispanics and blue-collar workers; whereas treatment group members had a greater proportion of white-collar workers and persons with post-high school education.

Nonresponse Bias in Program Impact Estimates

Although tables 3A1.1 and 3A1.2 suggest that survey-based estimates may understate true impacts, it is not sufficient just to examine respondent versus nonrespondent differences when attempting to judge the likely magnitude of this bias. One must also account for the *magnitude* of the nonresponse rate and the extent to which regression-based impact estimates *control statistically* for relevant treatment and control group differences produced by survey nonresponse.

For example, if nonresponse were negligible (say 1 percent), then the survey sample and full sample would be almost identical, even if there were large differences between respondents and nonrespondents: hence, response bias would be small. Furthermore, even if nonresponse were substantial (say 50 percent) and treatment and control group differences in respondent and nonrespondent differences were noticeable, the effect of survey nonresponse on program impact estimates would be small if these differences were controlled for by the regression models used to produce program impact estimates.

Perhaps the simplest way to explore the net effect of all of these factors is to compare regression-based impact estimates for the survey sample with those for the full sample, using the same UI-based outcome measures for both. If survey sample impact estimates for UI-based outcomes are markedly less favorable than those for the full sample, impact estimates based on survey outcome data (which are only available for the survey sample) probably understate true impacts substantially. On the other hand, if regression-adjusted UI-based impact estimates are roughly the same for the survey and full samples, then the net effect of nonresponse is probably small.

Table 3A1.3 presents findings for the two outcome measures used to compare survey respondents and nonrespondents. For men, program impacts on annual UI-reported follow-up earnings were $471 for the full sample, but only $27 for the survey sample, although neither finding was statistically significant. This difference equals roughly 6 percent of full-sample control group earnings. There was virtually no difference between survey-sample and full-sample UI-benefit impact estimates, however. For El Paso women, there was a much smaller difference between survey- and full-sample impacts on earnings, and there was little difference between survey- and full-sample UI benefit impact estimates. On balance then, it appears that survey-based estimates for men may understate true earnings impacts slightly, but for women this bias is probably negligible.

Table 3A1.3
Treatment Group Impact Estimates for the Survey Sample
Versus the Full Sample
(Dollars)

Impact	Survey sample	Full sample
All men		
Annual UI earnings	27	471
30-week UI benefits	–138*	–143*
El Paso women		
Annual UI earnings	809**	987**
30-week UI benefits	–209**	–193**

* or **=statistically significant at the 0.05 or 0.01 level, one-tail.

NOTE

1. Due to missing data for some items on some application forms, not all background characteristics were available for every sample member.
2. The fact that male survey respondents received more UI benefits than nonrespondents does not accord with the fact that respondents earned more. But the fact that treatment group respondents received relatively more UI benefits than control group respondents is consistent with the fact that treatment group respondents earned relatively less than control group respondents.

Appendix 3.2
Cross-Validating UI and Survey Employment Measures

Issues

The follow-up survey was designed to supplement UI records by providing additional outcome measures. But for one outcome, employment, it was possible to develop corresponding measures from *both* data sources; hence, a limited *cross-validation* was possible. For this purpose, UI records and follow-up survey responses were used to measure the percentage of sample members who were employed during their third and fourth follow-up quarters. These measures were compared for sample members for whom both were available.

UI employment measures for the third and fourth follow-up quarters were constructed by counting anyone with reported earnings during a quarter as employed. If no earnings were reported, the individual was counted as not employed. Survey data were used to compute employment rates as follows. Respondents were asked how many weeks they had worked during months 6–9 and months 10–12 after they were randomly assigned. All months were identified by name. Respondents with any weeks worked during months 6–9 were counted as employed during their third follow-up quarter. Respondents with any weeks worked during months 10–12 were counted as employed during their fourth follow-up quarter.

Because UI wage records are reported by calendar quarter, the third and fourth follow-up quarters from this source are not precisely three and four quarters after random assignment. Given that random assignment was continuous over time, it occurred on average in the middle of the random assignment quarter. Thus the first UI follow-up quarter for a typical sample member began roughly six to seven weeks after random assignment. Subsequent UI follow-up quarters were displaced equally in time. Because typical sample members were randomly assigned in the middle of their assignment month, there was a two-week lag between the beginning of their true third (or fourth) post-assignment quarter and its follow-up survey counterpart. Hence, UI follow-up quarters, which lagged by six to seven weeks, were four to five weeks later than survey follow-up quarters, which lagged by two weeks. Nevertheless, because follow-up quarters from both data sources overlapped for two out of three months, they provide a useful basis for comparison.

Findings

Now consider the findings in table 3A2.1. For the third follow-up quarter, employment rates from the two data sources were not consistently different.

61

UI employment measures were higher for half of the 14 experimental groups and survey measures were higher for the other half. This situation differed for men and women, but there was no clear evidence of systematic under-reporting by either data source. Instead, differences appear to reflect random measurement error.[1]

Table 3A2.1

Percent Employed During the Third and Fourth Follow-Up Quarters from UI Versus Survey Data for Sample Members With Both Data

		Third quarter[a]		Fourth quarter[a]	
		UI	Survey	UI	Survey
Men					
TEC/HCC	I	64	87	62	90
	I/II	64	76	57	81
	Control	69	70	64	78
SEE	I/II	56	62	58	73
	Control	63	60	60	72
SER/JOBS	I/II	65	73	48	68
	Control	77	72	60	84
Women					
TEC/HCC	I	68	81	62	76
	I/II	61	64	64	75
	Control	76	74	76	74
SEE	I/II	77	72	61	79
	Control	63	60	63	67
SER/JOBS	I/II	73	72	37	72
	Control	69	56	48	70

a. Survey quarters are four to five weeks earlier than UI quarters.

But a problem appears to exist during the fourth follow-up quarter. Specifically, UI employment measures were lower than their survey counterparts for all 14 experimental groups. Furthermore, the pattern of employment over time was completely different for the two data sources. Survey employment measures *increased* from the third to fourth follow-up quarter for 10 out of 14 experimental groups, whereas UI employment measures *decreased* for 10 out of 14 groups; hence, the fourth-quarter picture looked much bleaker UI measures.

The most likely explanation for this discrepancy is UI underreporting of fourth-quarter employment due to lags in employer wage reports to the state. Fourth follow-up quarter data were the most recent information available from UI at the time the study was completed. These data represent the third quarter of 1985 and were obtained from the state in April 1986. It is therefore likely that some employer reports had not yet been received or processed; thus earnings and employment may be understated by UI data for this quarter. Results based on fourth follow-up quarter UI data therefore should be interpreted with caution.

NOTE

1. One qualification to this conclusion arises from the fact that UI follow-up quarters are later than their survey-based counterparts. If employment rates were rising continually over time, as displaced sample members became reemployed, then UI employment measures, which are later, should be higher than survey-based employment measures. Hence, the fact that UI measures are only higher for half of the groups is consistent with some underreporting of employment by UI records.

4

The Sample

This chapter describes the Worker Adjustment Demonstration sample. Specifically, it describes the sample's size and composition, compares the sample with two related local groups, examines the economic displacement of sample members, and explores the comparability of treatment and control groups.

Sample Size

During the study, 2,259 persons were randomly assigned to treatment and control groups at the three demonstration sites. Follow-up information was obtained for 2,192 (97 percent) of these persons.[1] This group, referred to hereafter as the *experimental sample*, contained 1,366 men and 826 women (table 4.1). Sample sizes were smallest for women at TEC/HCC, and these groups were not initially comparable; hence, they were not used for impact analyses. All other subsamples were used, however.

Sample Background Characteristics

Table 4.2 describes the types of persons included in the experimental sample. As can be seen, this group comprised mainly prime working-age adults who had lost full-time jobs that paid well above the $3.35 federal minimum wage and had lasted for 2.4 to 5.3 years. Because of these prior work histories, almost all sample members (98 to 100 percent) were eligible for UI benefits. Indeed, the vast majority (69 to 96 percent) were receiving UI benefits when they applied to the demonstration program. Most of the remainder had already exhausted the benefits to which they were entitled.[2] In addition, 65 to 74 percent of the sample had one or more dependent children. In short, the typical

Worker Adjustment Demonstration sample member was an experienced worker who recently had lost a relatively good job and was using the UI system to help meet substantial family responsibilities.

Table 4.1
Experimental Sample Sizes

		Men	Women	Total
TEC/HCC I		266	55	321
	I/II	368	89	457
	Control	198	50	248
	Total	832	194	1,026
SEE	I/II	125	169	294
	Control	102	134	236
	Total	227	303	530
SER/JOBS I/II		156	180	336
	Control	151	149	300
	Total	307	329	636
Total		1,366	826	2,192

Within this group there were striking variations across sites, which reflected differences between the Houston and El Paso economies, as well as differences in site targeting strategies. TEC/HCC's sample was the most ethnically diverse. Roughly 52 to 57 percent of its participants were white, 20 to 36 percent were black, and 12 to 23 percent comprised other minorities, including Hispanics. In contrast, 96 to 98 percent of the SER/JOBS sample and 85 to 89 percent of the SEE sample were Hispanic, reflecting the predominantly Hispanic El Paso population.

A second major difference between the Houston and El Paso samples was their education levels. In Houston, between 56 and 67 percent of the TEC/HCC sample had some post-high school training; only 4 to 7 percent were school dropouts. In El Paso, however, 65 to 78 percent of the SER/JOBS sample were school dropouts, and only 4 to 8 percent had formal education beyond high school. In addition, many of these sample members may have received their education in Mexico, and thus probably had limited English speaking and writing ability.

SEE was between the two extremes represented by TEC/HCC and SER/JOBS. This reflected tradeoffs between its educational requirements as a private proprietary school and the limited backgrounds of its potential client pool.

Educational differences across sites also were reflected by differences in prior jobs. TEC/HCC prior jobs paid from $375 to $545 a week, or $9.52 to $13.41 an hour. This was several times the $174 to $228 weekly wage or $4.36 to $5.77 hourly wage for SEE and SER/JOBS. These differences were consistent with the occupational mix of each sample. Between 57 and 77 percent of the TEC/HCC sample had previously held white-collar jobs, compared to 7 to 23 percent for SEE and SER/JOBS. As a result, average TEC/HCC family income was roughly twice that of SEE and SER/JOBS ($17,600 to $20,300 versus $6,500 to $11,400).

Last, note that TEC/HCC served a greater proportion of UI exhaustees than either SEE or SER/JOBS, even though all three sites recruited applicants mainly from UI offices. Discussions with TEC/HCC staff suggest that its greater willingness to serve UI exhaustees reflected its lesser concern about meeting demonstration resource matching requirements. This may have been due to the fact that TEC/HCC had better access to matching funds. In summary, TEC/HCC sample members were more ethnically diverse, better educated, more highly paid, more frequently white-collar, and more often UI exhaustees than their El Paso counterparts. SER/JOBS was at the opposite extreme in virtually all regards. SEE was between these extremes, but more like SER/JOBS than TEC/HCC.

Table 4.2 also compares background characteristics for men and women in the sample. Perhaps most striking is the fact that women from all three sites had much lower prior earnings than men. At TEC/HCC prior weekly earnings for women were 65 percent of those for men; at SEE they were 71 percent; and at SER/JOBS they were 76 percent. Family income also was correspondingly lower for women than for men. These differences are consistent with prior research (e.g., Bassi 1984;

Table 4.2
Sample Background Characteristics

	Men			Women		
	TEC/HCC	SEE	SER/JOBS	TEC/HCC	SEE	SER/JOBS
Ethnicity (%)						
White (non-Hispanic)	57	11	3	52	8	0
Black (non-Hispanic)	20	4	1	36	1	1
Hispanic	10	85	96	5	89	98
Other	13	0	0	7	2	1
Education (%)						
<12	7	36	65	4	58	78
12	27	43	27	40	30	19
>12	67	21	8	56	12	4
Prior occupation (%)						
White-collar	57	22	12	77	23	7
Blue-collar	39	59	68	19	71	87
UI status (%)						
Eligible	100	98	99	100	98	100
Recipient	69	70	96	72	85	95
Exhaustee	18	13	3	20	5	3

Family status (%)						
Any children	66	65	71	68	71	74
Child <6	25	36	39	17	32	30
Age (%)						
<35	37	62	50	43	52	47
35–54	55	31	40	52	44	46
>54	9	6	10	5	5	7
Layoff job (mean)						
Weekly wage ($)	545	226	228	375	184	174
Hourly wage ($)	13.41	5.77	5.66	9.52	4.73	4.36
Weekly hours	40	39	40	38	39	40
Years held	3.8	2.4	4.6	4.0	3.9	5.3
Family income (mean $)	20,300	10,500	8,100	17,600	11,400	6,500

NOTE: Sample sizes vary due to missing data for certain items.

Bloom 1987b), and supports the decision to report program impacts separately for men and women.

Economic Displacement of the Sample

JTPA Title III, which funded the demonstration, provides broad guidelines for identifying displaced workers to serve. These guidelines are intended to focus on persons who have permanently lost stable, well-paying jobs due to forces beyond their control, such as changing technology or increased international competition.

Prior attempts to identify displaced workers have relied on measures such as layoff-job duration and wage rate, laid-off worker age, and layoff-job status, i.e., whether it was in a declining industry, occupation or region (Bendick and Devine 1981; Sheingold 1982; Flaim and Sehgal 1985). All of these measures are proxies, however, for the following:

1. Long-term prior employment in a good job
2. Probable sustained unemployment after layoff
3. Probable reduced future wages after reemployment

Table 4.3 illustrates the extent to which Worker Adjustment Demonstration sample members met these criteria by focusing on control group pre- and post-layoff experiences. Control group experiences were used because they reflect what treatment group experiences would have been without the demonstration.

First, consider the quality of prior control group jobs. These jobs paid well above the prevailing $3.35 federal minimum wage. Mean sample wage rates ranged from a low of $4.31 for women at SER/JOBS to a high of $12.54 for men at TEC/HCC. Median wage rates were $4.36 to $12.00. Also note that the duration of prior control group employment was substantial, ranging from a mean of 2.6 years for men at SEE to 5.6 years for women at SER/JOBS. Median durations ranged from 1.1 to 3.9 years.[3] Hence, the demonstration sample in general— and the Houston subsample in particular—differed from *disadvantaged persons* who cannot find or maintain decent jobs.[4]

Table 4.3
Control Group Layoff-Job Characteristics
and Reemployment Experience

	TEC/HCC	SEE	SER/JOBS
Men			
Layoff job			
Mean years duration	3.5	2.6	4.4
Median years duration	1.1	1.5	2.4
Mean hourly wage ($)	12.54	5.93	5.58
Median hourly wage ($)	12.00	5.20	4.92
Reemployment rate (%)			
UI records	78	83	80
Follow-up survey	84	74	88
Wage replacement rate (%)	101	95	95
Women			
Layoff job			
Mean years duration	2.9	3.6	5.6
Median years duration	2.5	2.8	3.9
Mean hourly wage ($)	8.85	4.62	4.31
Median hourly wage ($)	8.37	4.50	4.36
Reemployment rate (%)			
UI records	83	77	81
Follow-up survey	81	72	75
Wage replacement rate (%)	74	90	86

Next, consider the ability of control group members to find new jobs. Table 4.3 presents two measures of their reemployment success. The first measure is the percentage of controls who became reemployed during the year after random assignment, according to UI wage records. Roughly 80 percent of the control group became reemployed and 20 percent did not: hence, a substantial portion of the sample suffered serious reemployment problems. Note, however, that not all legal jobs in Texas were covered by UI at the time, although over 90 percent were. Therefore, UI reemployment measures may have missed some control group jobs and, consequently, may overstate their reemployment problems slightly.

A second reemployment measure was constructed from follow-up survey responses. This measure was defined as the percentage of controls who reported some weeks worked during their third or fourth follow-up quarters. Table 4.3 indicates that roughly 80 percent reported some work, whereas 20 percent reported none. A few survey respondents may have found and lost jobs during their first two follow-up quarters, however. Thus, the survey-based reemployment measure also may overstate control group reemployment problems. Given the nature of the UI and survey data used, and the striking findings they present, however, it appears that control group members did indeed experience serious reemployment problems.

Last, consider the extent to which controls who became reemployed regained their prior wages. This outcome was measured in terms of wage replacement rates. Wage replacement rates were computed as the ratio of hourly reemployment wages to hourly layoff-job wages, in percent. Reemployment wages were defined as those reported by survey respondents for the follow-up survey week, one year after random assignment.[5] Layoff-job wages were obtained from program application forms.

Note that five out of six control groups had wage replacement rates of less than 100 percent; hence, their reemployment wages were less than what they had earned previously. Because these figures were in current rather than constant dollars, they do not reflect additional real wage losses due to inflation; thus, real wage replacement rates are even lower than those reported in the table.

In summary, their best available evidence suggests that control group members lost good jobs, were unemployed for a long time, and experienced reemployment wage losses. In short, they were *displaced workers*.

The Sample Versus Other Local Target Groups

To further place the experimental sample in perspective, tables 4.4 and 4.5 compare its characteristics with those of all local unemployed persons who were insured by UI, and all adult JTPA Title II-A participants.

The insured unemployed represent a broad cross-section of laid-off workers in a locality; hence, comparing the demonstration sample with this group illustrates the extent to which sites served specific laid-off worker subgroups. Title II-A participants reflect the backgrounds of disadvantaged persons at each site. Comparing the demonstration sample with this group illustrates the extent to which sites made the intended distinction between JTPA Title III programs for displaced workers and JTPA Title II-A programs for disadvantaged persons. Now consider the findings.

Relative to all insured unemployed, TEC/HCC oversampled men; professional, technical, and management occupations; and jobs in the petroleum and primary and fabricated metals and machinery industries. Hence, the TEC/HCC sample represents a narrow segment of the Houston laid-off worker population.

Relative to adult Title II-A participants, the TEC/HCC sample had much higher education levels. In addition, based on UI status, it appears that the TEC/HCC group had greater prior employment. Thus, TEC/HCC sharply distinguished its clients from disadvantaged persons.

Now consider these comparisons for SEE and SER/JOBS. In terms of demographic characteristics, sex, ethnicity, and age, samples from both sites reflected the existing local pool of insured unemployed. The main differences were SER/JOBS' emphasis on persons laid off from jobs in apparel manufacturing, and SEE's emphasis on persons laid off in other manufacturing areas—mostly electronics and electrical products. In general, however, the SEE and SER/JOBS samples were not as narrowly targeted as their TEC/HCC counterparts.

Relative to adult Title II-A participants, the SEE and SER/JOBS samples had much higher rates of UI participation, and thus, probably had more extensive prior employment. This is consistent with the dif-

Table 4.4
The Demonstration Sample Versus the Insured Unemployed
Versus JTPA II-A Participants
(Houston)

	TEC/HCC sample	Insured unemployed	City adult II-A	County adult II-A
Male (%)	81	64	42	46
Ethnicity (%)				
White (non-Hispanic)	56	51	13	52
Black (non-Hispanic)	23	--	62	27
Hispanic	9	--	20	19
Other	11	--	5	3
Education (%)				
<12	4	--	13	23
12	31	--	48	41
>12	65	--	39	36
UI status (%)				
Recipient	70	--	10	20
Exhaustee	19	--	11	8
Prior occupation[a] (%)				
Professional, technical, managerial	49	8	--	--
Clerical, sales	12	26	--	--

Service	<1	7	--	--
Machine trades	16	8	--	--
Benchwork	2	2	--	--
Structural	13	21	--	--
Miscellaneous	7	12	--	--
Prior industry[a] (%)				
Mining	10	4	--	--
Construction	14	23	--	--
Manufacturing	32	18	--	--
Apparel	0	<1	--	--
Petroleum refining	8	1	--	--
Primary & fabricated metals, machinery	21	10	--	--
Other	4	7	--	--
Wholesale/retail	7	22	--	--
Services	16	19	--	--
Other	21	13	--	--
Age (%)				
<22	<1	4	--	--
22–54	92	86	98	97
>54	8	10	2	3

a. Missing industry or occupation not included.

Table 4.5
The Demonstration Sample Versus the Insured Unemployed
Versus JTPA II-A Participants
(El Paso)

	SEE sample	SER/JOBS sample	Insured unemployed	Adult II-A[a]
Male (%)	44	47	46	44
Ethnicity (%)				
White (non-Hispanic)	9	2	12	11
Black (non-Hispanic)	3	<1	--	6
Hispanic	87	97	--	82
Other	1	<1	--	1
Education (%)				
<12	43	70	--	27
12	41	24	--	38
>12	17	6	--	35
UI status (%)				
Recipient	77	96	--	10
Exhaustee	9	3	--	7
Prior occupation[b] (%)				
Professional, technical, managerial	5	2	1	--
Clerical, sales	18	8	18	--

Service	5	5	9	--
Machine trades	8	10	4	--
Benchwork	40	50	38	--
Structural	12	15	11	--
Miscellaneous	12	11	12	--
Prior industry[b] (%)				
Mining	<1	<1	<1	--
Construction	8	13	8	--
Manufacturing	76	83	53	--
Apparel	34	62	36	--
Petroleum refining	<1	0	0	--
Primary & fabricated metals, machinery	3	1	3	--
Other	39	20	14	--
Wholesale/retail	4	1	13	--
Services	8	0	12	--
Other	4	3	7	--
Age (%)				
<22	3	5	5	--
22–54	92	86	86	98
>54	6	9	8	2

a. Upper Rio Grande Service Delivery Area.
b. Missing industry or occupation not included.

Table 4.6
Treatment and Control Group Characteristics
(Men)

	TEC/HCC I	TEC/HCC I/II	TEC/HCC control	SEE I/II	SEE control	SER/JOBS I/II	SER/JOBS control
Ethnicity (%)							
White (non-Hispanic)	61	55	58	13	8	4	2
Black (non-Hispanic)	20	23	17	2	6	1	1
Hispanic	11	8	11	84	85	95	97
Other	8	14	14	1	1	0	0
Education (%)							
<12	6	5*	10	32	41	67	64
12	27	29	23	49*	34	26	28
>12	67	66	67	19	25	8	9
Layoff job (%)							
White-collar	58	56	57	25	18	10	15
Blue-collar	40	38	39	51*	68	66	70
UI status (%)							
Eligible	100	99	100	99	97	99	99
Recipient	70	69	69	73	66	96	95
Exhaustee	19	19	18	10	16	5*	1

Family status (%)							
Any children	67	65	64	68	62	70	73
Child <6	21	29	24	39	32	39	39
Age (%)							
<35	36	38	36	66	58	51	49
35–54	55	55	54	32	31	37	42
>54	9	8	10	2**	11	12	9
Layoff job (mean)							
Weekly wage ($)	591**	535	503	220	234	229	226
Hourly wage ($)	14.48**	13.12	12.54	5.65	5.93	5.73	5.58
Weekly hours	41	41	40	39	39	40	40
Years held	4.2	3.7	3.5	2.2	2.6	4.8	4.4
Family income (mean $)	20,400	20,100	20,500	11,000	9,800	8,100	8,100

NOTE: Sample sizes vary due to missing data for certain items.
* or **=statistically significant treatment and control group difference at the 0.05 or 0.01 level, two-tail.

Table 4.7
Treatment and Control Group Characteristics
(Women)

	TEC/HCC I	TEC/HCC I/II	TEC/HCC control	SEE I/II	SEE control	SER/JOBS I/II	SER/JOBS control
Ethnicity (%)							
White (non-Hispanic)	53	56	44	8	8	0	1
Black (non-Hispanic)	29	36	42	1	1	1	0
Hispanic	5	4	4	89	90	97	99
Other	13	4	10	2	1	2	0
Education (%)							
<12	4	3	6	60	55	77	78
12	40	37	44	30	30	19	18
>12	56	60	50	10	16	4	4
Layoff job (%)							
White-collar	75	73	86	23	24	7	7
Blue-collar	21	22	12	70	71	87	86
UI status (%)							
Eligible	98	100	100	98	97	99	100
Recipient	80	70	68	83	89	97	93
Exhaustee	15	21	24	3	8	2	5

Family status (%)							
Any children	62	72	66	71	71	69	79
Child <6	15	18	18	30	35	30	31
Age (%)							
<35	53	36	44	50	54	49	44
35–54	41	58	54	45	41	44	48
>54	5	7	2	5	5	7	9
Layoff job (mean)							
Weekly wage ($)	366	391	359	189	177	176	172
Hourly wage ($)	9.44	9.98	8.85	4.81	4.62	4.40	4.31
Weekly hours	38	39	38	39	38	40	40
Years held	4.2	4.4	2.9	4.1	3.6	5.0	5.6
Family income (mean $)	18,000	16,600	18,700	11,500	11,200	6,400	6,600

NOTE: Sample sizes vary due to missing data for certain items. Also, no treatment and control differences were statistically significant at the 0.05 level, two-tail.

ference one would expect between displaced workers and disadvantaged persons. Surprisingly, however, both the SEE and SER/JOBS samples had less education than their Title II-A counterparts. This was especially true for SER/JOBS, where 70 percent of the demonstration sample were school dropouts. Thus, the distinction between Title III and Title II-A was less clear in El Paso than in Houston.

Treatment and Control Group Comparability

As indicated previously, the purpose of random assignment is to produce comparable treatment and control groups. Doing so ensures that subsequent outcome differences reflect true program impacts, not initial differences between the groups involved. However, one can never be sure that random assignment was not compromised in some unknown way. Moreover, even if random assignment was not compromised, it is possible to get a *bad draw*, that produces noncomparable treatment and control groups by chance.[6]

To explore this issue for a specific sample, one can compare treatment and control group background characteristics. If substantial differences exist, this suggests—but does not prove—that important unobserved differences also may exist. If no major differences are observed, this suggests—but does not prove—that no important unobserved differences exist.

Tables 4.6 and 4.7 provide such a comparison for the Worker Adjustment Demonstration sample. As can be seen, there is a consistently high degree of treatment and control group comparability. Using conventional standards, only seven out of 88 treatment and control group differences were statistically significant for men (table 4.6); and none were significant for women (table 4.7).[7] In short, almost all differences were within the bounds of random sampling error, and few were large in magnitude. The only exception to this rule was the subsample of women from TEC/HCC. As can be seen, there were substantial treatment and control differences for this group. Because of the very small samples involved, however, these differences were not statistically significant. Nevertheless, because these differences (and others discussed in later chapters) were quite large, women from TEC/HCC were not included in program impact estimates.

On balance then, to the extent that one can determine from existing data, it appears that with one exception, the Worker Adjustment Demonstration produced highly comparable treatment and control groups, which, in turn, provide the basis for unbiased program impact estimates.

NOTES

1. The 67 missing assignees were distributed across all treatment and control groups.

2. The maximum duration of regular UI benefits was 26 weeks. Extended benefits were available for six to eight additional weeks at the time.

3. Mean earnings and layoff job duration were higher than medians because the magnitudes of unusually high wages and job durations (*outliers*) influenced the values of means but not medians. Both summary statistics tell roughly the same story, however.

4. JTPA Title II-A serves economically disadvantaged persons.

5. Reemployment wages only cover jobs held during the follow-up survey week; they do not cover jobs held and lost before then.

6. The larger the sample, the smaller the probability of a substantial *bad draw*.

7. Statistical significance was determined at the 0.05 level using a two-tail test.

Part II

Findings

The four chapters in this section present evaluation findings from the Texas Worker Adjustment Demonstration. Chapter 5 describes patterns of participation among treatment group members; chapter 6 compares treatment and control group labor market experiences; chapter 7 presents program impact estimates; chapter 8 compares program impacts and costs and summarizes study findings.

5
Participation
and Services Received

Chapter 5 examines patterns of participation in the Worker Adjustment Demonstration and specifically addresses the following questions:

1. What fraction of each treatment group actually participated?
2. How did participants differ from no-shows?
3. What fraction of the Tier I/II treatment group received Tier II services and what was their mix of classroom training versus OJT?
4. How did Tier II participants differ from Tier I Only participants?
5. How long were participants enrolled in the program, and how did their length of stay vary by site and program activity?

Participation

Issues

JTPA Title III programs recruit individuals and provide them with an opportunity to receive services, but these programs cannot mandate participation. Consequently, only a portion of the eligible population applies to the program, and only a fraction of these applicants ultimately participate. Furthermore, different participants receive different services. This sequential multistage selection process reflects the outcomes of individual choices made by potential clients, as they compare the benefits and costs of their program options with each other, and with nonprogram alternatives. Simultaneously, it reflects decisions made by program staff, as they screen applicants and attempt to tailor a program that matches their needs, interests, and abilities.

Unfortunately, little is known about the factors that influence participation; however, such information is extremely important in helping program staff effectively use their limited recruitment resources.

As a first step toward a theory of program participation, it is useful to conceptualize its major determinants in three broad categories:

1. program intake procedures
2. program services
3. program applicants

In terms of *program intake*:

1. The more time elapsed between initial applicant contact and receipt of program services, the greater the perceived cost of participation and the more distant its perceived benefits; hence, the lower the participation rate;
2. The more appointments required for intake and the more separate locations applicants must find, the greater the effort required by them and the greater the potential for confusion; hence, the lower the participation rate;
3. The more documentation required from applicants to determine their eligibility, the greater the cost to them of participating; hence, the lower the participation rate;
4. The sooner applicants learn about program benefits, the sooner they will begin to appreciate its benefits to them, and the greater their enthusiasm will be; hence, the higher the participation rate;
5. The better the match between applicants' backgrounds (e.g., their culture and social class), the physical surroundings and location of the program, and the backgrounds of its staff, the more comfortable applicants will be; hence, the higher the participation rate;
6. The more vigorously program staff promote participation, the greater its perceived benefits will be; hence, the higher the participation rate.

In terms of *program services*:

1. The more extensive the services, the greater their perceived benefits; hence, the higher participation will be. This implies that applicants who are eligible for Tier I/II will be more likely to participate than those who are eligible for Tier I only.[1]
2. The better the match between applicants' backgrounds and program offerings, the more comfortable applicants will feel and the

more benefits they will perceive; hence, the greater participation will be.

3. The more extensive the support services (especially for child care and income maintenance), the more feasible it will be for individuals to participate; hence, the greater participation will be.[2]

In terms of *program applicants*:

1. Persons with more viable alternatives (especially job prospects) will be less likely to participate.
2. Persons with stronger motivation will be more likely to participate.
3. Persons with greater financial resources can better afford to participate, and thus will be more likely to do so.
4. Persons with greater family responsibilities can less well afford to participate, and thus will be less likely to do so.
5. Persons who have been unemployed for a brief period may expect to return to their jobs and thus may not wish to participate.
6. Persons who have been unemployed for a very long time may become too discouraged to participate.

Participation in the Demonstration

Worker Adjustment Demonstration participants were defined as treatment group members who attended at least one day of program activities. Treatment group members who attended no activities were classified as no-shows.

Table 5.1 indicates that participation rates for the demonstration were quite high, ranging from 58 to 88 percent. To place this result in perspective, consider the experience of the Delaware and the Buffalo displaced worker experiments (Bloom 1987a; Corson, Long, and Maynard 1985), the only other experimental evaluations of displaced worker programs at the time the present study was conducted.[3]

The Delaware experiment, which had a 75-percent participation rate, recruited UI recipients who had been collecting benefits for seven to 12 consecutive weeks. In this respect, Delaware applicants were similar to the Worker Adjustment Demonstration sample. In contrast, the Buffalo demonstration used a broad range of recruitment strategies, yielding a very different sample. Its applicants had been laid off for roughly eight months, their UI benefits were exhausted, their savings probably were depleted, and they may have been too bitter to seek help from a government program. Consequently, only 26 percent participated.

Table 5.1
Participation Rates
(Percent)

	Men	Women
TEC/HCC I	62	58
TEC/HCC I/II	65	69
SEE I/II	65	76
SER/JOBS I/II	88	87

Now consider what can be learned from the variation in participation rates across Worker Adjustment Demonstration sites. TEC/HCC experienced the lowest rates—58 to 69 percent—which probably reflects three features of its intake process. First, applicants were required to make three separate trips to three different locations, each of which provided an opportunity for fallout to occur. The first trip was to a local TEC office, to apply and be screened for eligibility. Eligible applicants were then randomly assigned to treatment or control status by the evaluation contractor. The second trip (for treatment group members only) was to the TEC demonstration headquarters for an interview and orientation session. The third trip was to Career Circles to begin job-search assistance.

A second feature of TEC/HCC intake that may have affected participation was that applicants received little information about the program when they applied (at a local TEC office). Furthermore, they did not meet program staff until their second trip (to the TEC demonstration headquarters); thus, their early incentives to proceed were limited.

A third important factor was the elapsed time between application and participation. This period was almost never less than a week; thus, many opportunities to preempt applicants' participation—including their finding a job—could and did occur.

One further point about TEC/HCC is its lack of a *clear* difference between participation in Tier I only and Tier I/II. Substantially greater participation was expected for Tier I/II, the more extensive and presumably more desirable option. This did not materialize, however, perhaps because of the mismatch between the blue-collar Tier II activities at TEC/HCC and its predominantly white-collar participants.

SER/JOBS was at the opposite extreme in terms of participation rates. Almost 90 percent of its treatment group received services, the main reason probably being project staff's vigorous and sustained effort to remain in contact with treatment group members. This expression of personal concern reflected the activist role of SER/JOBS as an advocate for the Hispanic community.

A second probable reason for SER/JOBS' high participation rate stemmed from the fact that staff and applicants shared a distinct ethnic and cultural background; both were almost exclusively Hispanic. Therefore, it may have been easier for an early rapport to develop. In addition, the extensive documentation required for applicants to establish their eligibility probably screened out persons with weak motivation *before* random assignment. Finally, all application and screening took place in the SER/JOBS demonstration office and was conducted by its demonstration staff, enabling applicants to learn about program benefits and meet staff early in this process.

SEE participation rates fell between those for SER/JOBS and TEC/HCC. They were higher than TEC/HCC, probably because of SEE's centralized—and therefore brief—intake process. Intake was conducted in a demonstration office by program staff, and required extensive documentation from applicants prior to random assignment. SEE participation rates were lower than those for SER/JOBS, perhaps because of differences in the extent to which its staff followed up applicants who did not attend program activities.

Participants Versus No-Shows

Tables 5.2–5.4 compare the background characteristics of Worker Adjustment Demonstration participants and no-shows. Note that the only

Table 5.2
Participant Versus No-Show Background Characteristics
(Houston Men)

	TEC/HCC I		TEC/HCC I/II	
	Participants	**No-Shows**	**Participants**	**No-Shows**
Ethnicity (%)				
White (non-Hispanic)	61	60	55	54
Black (non-Hispanic)	21	18	21	25
Hispanic	9	14	8	9
Education (%)				
< 12	4	10	5	7
12	22	34	24	38
> 12	74	56	72	55
Layoff job (%)				
White-collar	62	50	64	41
Blue-collar	35	48	31	51
UI status (%)				
Recipient	74	64	68	71
Exhaustee	18	21	18	19
Family status (%)				
Any children	68	64	66	63
Child < 6	19	26	25	36
Age (%)				
< 35	31	44	34	45
35–54	58	52	55	52
> 54	11	5	11	3
Layoff job (mean)				
Weekly wage ($)	622	541	538	528
Hourly wage ($)	15.42	12.93	13.42	12.57
Years held	4.5	3.7	3.8	3.5
Prior (mean)				
Quarterly earnings ($)	4,379	3,728	3,834	3,504
Annual family income ($)	22,100	17,530	21,230	17,970

consistent difference across sites was that participants' had held prior jobs much longer than no-shows. Participants, therefore, probably had more stable and/or more extensive prior employment experience, and thereby may have perceived greater immediate benefits from job-search assistance—the first and main component of programs at all three sites.

In all other respects, participation patterns differed markedly across sites. This does not mean, however, that participation decisions were random. On the contrary, a careful reading of tables 5.2– 5.4 suggests that *participation was a function of the match between applicants' backgrounds and program characteristics.*

This point is best illustrated by comparing findings for men at TEC/HCC and SER/JOBS. Recall that all TEC/HCC participants started their program with an intensive, week-long job-search component operated by a private firm, Career Circles, Inc. This initial activity was located in an exclusive shopping mall; it employed sophisticated written exercises; it emphasized introspection and career exploration; and it promoted self-employment. Thus, Career Circles was most appropriate for educated, experienced, white-collar professionals.

Not unexpectedly, table 5.2 indicates that male TEC/HCC participants were more likely to have post-high school educations, were more likely to be white-collar workers, had higher previous wages, and had higher incomes than corresponding no-shows. In contrast, SER/JOBS (table 5.3) was an Hispanic community-based organization that historically served low-income, disadvantaged persons. The SER/JOBS Worker Adjustment Demonstration required little formal education; it was conducted in both Spanish and English; it emphasized immediate reemployment; and it was staffed almost solely by Hispanics. Consequently, male SER/JOBS participants were more likely to be Hispanics, high school dropouts, and blue-collar workers (table 5.3). In addition, they had lower prior wages and lower previous incomes than no-shows.

SEE was a private, for-profit, vocational education institution. It historically provided tuition-based courses for the general public in El Paso; hence, its Worker Adjustment Demonstration was less focused on a specific subpopulation. Consequently, there was no consistent difference between its male participants and no-shows (table 5.3).

Table 5.3
Participant Versus No-Show Background Characteristics
(El Paso Men)

	SEE I/II		SER/JOBS I/II	
	Participants	**No-Shows**	**Participants**	**No-Shows**
Ethnicity (%)				
White (non-Hispanic)	9	20	3	11
Black (non-Hispanic)	2	2	0	5
Hispanic	88	77	97	79
Education (%)				
<12	35	28	68	58
12	46	56	26	26
>12	20	16	7	16
Layoff job (%)				
White-collar	25	26	10	11
Blue-collar	48	59	68	50
UI status (%)				
Recipient	74	69	96	94
Exhaustee	9	12	5	6
Family status (%)				
Any children	69	66	71	63
Child <6	37	43	39	37
Age (%)				
<35	67	64	50	63
35–54	30	36	37	37
>54	4	0	13	0
Layoff job (mean)				
Weekly wage ($)	214	234	223	273
Hourly wage ($)	5.56	5.88	5.58	6.82
Years held	2.5	1.4	4.9	3.8
Prior (mean)				
Quarterly earnings ($)	1,807	1,731	1,768	1,545
Annual family income ($)	10,810	11,550	7,990	8,730

Table 5.4
Participant Versus No-Show Background Characteristics
(El Paso Women)

	SEE I/II		SER/JOBS I/II	
	Participants	No-Shows	Participants	No-Shows
Ethnicity (%)				
White (non-Hispanic)	9	5	0	0
Black (non-Hispanic)	2	0	1	0
Hispanic	88	92	97	100
Education (%)				
< 12	61	58	78	75
12	32	24	18	25
> 12	7	18	4	0
Layoff job (%)				
White-collar	22	31	6	13
Blue-collar	73	58	88	83
UI status (%)				
Recipient	85	74	97	96
Exhaustee	4	0	2	4
Family status (%)				
Any children	71	73	69	71
Child < 6	30	28	31	25
Age (%)				
< 35	50	47	50	46
35–54	45	48	43	46
> 54	5	5	6	8
Layoff job (mean)				
Weekly wage ($)	192	178	177	170
Hourly wage ($)	4.85	4.69	4.43	4.24
Years held	4.5	2.9	5.4	2.4
Prior (mean)				
Quarterly earnings ($)	1,886	1,750	1,477	1,506
Annual family income ($)	11,830	9,230	6,330	6,630

Now consider the findings for women at SEE and SER/JOBS (table 5.4). Almost all women at both sites were Hispanic, and at neither site was there a systematic difference between participants and no-shows. This result is consistent with that for men at SEE (where participants and no-shows were quite similar) but inconsistent with that for men at SER/JOBS (where participants differed appreciably from no-shows). One explanation for the apparent inconsistency at SER/JOBS is as follows.

For women, 97 to 100 percent of the SER/JOBS sample were Hispanic; 75 to 78 percent were school dropouts; and 83 to 88 percent had blue-collar backgrounds. Hence, there was little margin for systematic sorting into participants and no-shows along these dimensions. In contrast, the corresponding male treatment group was more diverse, and therefore had a greater margin for sorting.

Stepping back a moment, the general lesson that seems apparent from the preceding analysis is *that participation increases with the degree to which a program matches its applicants' backgrounds. In addition, the broader the applicant group, the greater the margin for sorting, and the more narrowly focused the program, the stronger the motivation for doing so.*

Services Received

Although each Worker Adjustment Demonstration site adopted the Tier I/II model specified by TDCA, they adapted it in ways that reflected local service availability and existing institutional arrangements. In addition, the needs, interests, and backgrounds of participants at each site were quite different; hence, the mix of services received varied. For example, only a small fraction of SER/JOBS Tier I/II participants received Tier II services; the overwhelming majority received job-search assistance only (table 5.5). In contrast, about half of the Tier I/II participants at SEE and TEC/HCC received Tier II services.

Among those participants who received some form of Tier II training, the type of training they received varied substantially across sites. For example, TEC/HCC provided classroom training for almost all Tier

II participants.[4] This reflected the fact that Houston Community College had the lead role for Tier II activities.

Table 5.5
Percent of Participants by Program Activity

	TEC/HCC I/II	SEE I/II	SER/JOBS I/II
Job-search only	56	43	74
Classroom training[a]	37	29	3
OJT[a]	7	28	23
Total	100	100	100

a. Job-search assistance was also received.

At the opposite extreme, SER/JOBS relied almost exclusively on OJT for Tier II. This reflected its emphasis on finding immediate reemployment for participants, in order to replace their lost incomes. Consequently, only 3 percent of SER/JOBS' participants received classroom training. SEE's Tier II mix was roughly half classroom training and half OJT. Its use of classroom training reflected an in-house capacity to provide this service, but its use of OJT reflected a willingness to reach beyond immediate in-house capabilities.

Now consider recipients of Tier II services at each site (table 5.6). First, note that women were considerably and consistently more likely than men to receive these services. Women were more likely to get classroom training at TEC/HCC (its predominant Tier II activity), OJT at SER/JOBS (its predominant Tier II activity), and both classroom training and OJT at SEE (with an equal mix of both).

It is not clear how much of this outcome reflected choices made by participants versus decisions made by program staff. For example, laid-off women may have been less likely to be sole earners in their households, and, therefore, may have had greater flexibility to participate in a more extended program. On the other hand, or in addition, site staff may have felt that laid-off women had less extensive and/or less transferable job skills than men. Hence, staff may have been more likely to channel women into job-skills training. Regardless of the factors that produced this situation, it is clear that all three sites used a human capital-building approach more frequently for women than for men.

Table 5.6
Percent of Male and Female Participants
by Program Activity

	Men	Women
TEC/HCC I/II		
Job-search only	59	46
Classroom training[a]	32	52
OJT[a]	9	2
Total	100	100
SEE I/II		
Job-search only	56	36
Classroom training[a]	24	31
OJT[a]	20	33
Total	100	100
SER/JOBS I/II		
Job-search only	78	71
Classroom training[a]	4	2
OJT[a]	18	27
Total	100	100

a. Job-search assistance was also received.

Tables 5.7 and 5.8 explore further potential differences among participants in each major program activity. Due to small sample sizes, female TEC/HCC participants, male TEC/HCC OJT participants, and

Table 5.7
Tier I/II Participant Background Characteristics by Program Activity
(Men)

	TEC/HCC I/II		SEE I/II			SER/JOBS I/II	
	Job-search only	Classroom training[a]	Job-search only	Classroom training[a]	OJT[a]	Job-search only	OJT[a]
Ethnicity (%)							
White (non-Hispanic)	59	48	7	10	13	4	0
Black (non-Hispanic)	14	33	2	5	0	0	0
Hispanic	10	5	89	85	87	96	100
Education (%)							
<12	4	6	44	25	19	71	52
12	20	27	40	40	69	25	28
>12	77	67	16	35	13	4	20
Layoff job (%)							
White-collar	71	56	16	47	20	8	17
Blue-collar	23	41	51	37	53	71	54
UI status (%)							
Recipient	69	68	77	63	81	95	100
Exhaustee	14	25	5	26	0	6	0
Family status (%)							
Any children	67	63	69	60	81	73	68
Child <6	28	15	36	35	44	37	60

Table 5.7 (continued)

	TEC/HCC I/II		SEE I/II			SER/JOBS I/II	
	Job-search only	Classroom training[a]	Job-search only	Classroom training[a]	OJT[a]	Job-search only	OJT[a]
Age (%)							
<35	33	35	56	80	81	46	68
35–54	54	55	38	20	19	40	28
>54	13	10	7	0	0	14	4
Layoff job (mean)							
Weekly wage ($)	569	473	225	208	193	232	191
Hourly wage ($)	14.03	12.07	5.79	5.62	4.87	5.81	4.77
Years held	3.5	4.8	2.6	2.3	2.7	5.5	2.5
Prior (mean)							
Quarterly earnings ($)	3,990	3,680	1,780	1,860	1,830	1,840	1,530
Annual family income ($)	23,010	18,130	8,860	15,310	10,740	7,940	7,510

a. Job-search assistance was also received.

Table 5.8
Tier I/II Participant Background Characteristics by Program Activity
(Women)

	SEE I/II			SER/JOBS I/II	
	Job-search only	Classroom training[a]	OJT[a]	Job-search only	OJT[a]
Ethnicity (%)					
White (non-Hispanic)	11	13	2	0	0
Black (non-Hispanic)	0	5	0	1	0
Hispanic	89	75	98	97	98
Education (%)					
<12	59	53	72	80	76
12	28	43	26	15	21
>12	13	5	2	5	2
Layoff job (%)					
White-collar	32	23	10	6	5
Blue-collar	59	74	86	86	93
UI status (%)					
Recipient	87	90	78	97	100
Exhaustee	0	3	10	3	0

Table 5.8 (continued)

	SEE I/II			SER/JOBS I/II	
	Job-search only	Classroom training[a]	OJT[a]	Job-search only	OJT[a]
Family status (%)					
Any children	61	73	79	68	71
Child <6	37	18	35	30	31
Age (%)					
<35	61	43	47	45	60
35–54	33	50	51	48	33
>54	7	8	2	6	7
Layoff job (mean)					
Weekly wage ($)	200	204	173	178	173
Hourly wage ($)	5.02	5.15	4.37	4.45	4.31
Years held	4.8	5.1	3.5	5.7	4.4
Prior (mean)					
Quarterly earnings ($)	1,820	2,360	1,490	1,390	1,690
Annual family income ($)	11,930	11,840	11,720	6,490	5,830

a. Job-search assistance was also received.

SER/JOBS classroom trainees were not included. The only clear pattern emerging from the tables was that men with higher prior wages were more likely to receive job-search assistance only. Higher wages may reflect more job experience and/or job skills; hence, persons with these characteristics may have tended to be channeled directly back into the job market.

Enrollment Duration

This final section briefly describes the duration of time that participants spent in the program.[5] As can be seen (table 5.9), the shortest program was at SER/JOBS, where participants were enrolled for 10 to 11 weeks, on average. This reflected staff emphasis on immediate reemployment. In contrast, programs at TEC/HCC and SEE were mainly 14 to 17 weeks long. It is particularly interesting to note that Tier I/II women were enrolled longer than Tier I/II men at all three sites. This probably reflects the fact that a greater proportion of women received Tier II services.

Table 5.9
Mean Weeks Enrolled by Participants

	Men	Women
TEC/HCC I	15	14
TEC/HCC I/II	17	23
SEE I/II	15	17
SER/JOBS I/II	10	11

Table 5.10 controls for this difference in Tier II service receipt by reporting separate enrollment periods for men and women by program activity. As can be seen, there is no remaining pronounced or consis-

tent difference by gender. There is, however, the expected difference between the times enrolled in Tier I Only and Tier I/II.

Table 5.10
Mean Weeks Enrolled by Participants in Program Activities

	Job-search only	Classroom training[a]	OJT[a]
Men			
TEC/HCC I	15		
TEC/HCC I/II	12	23	**
SEE I/II	13	15	19
SER/JOBS I/II	8	**	13
Women			
TEC/HCC I	14		
TEC/HCC I/II	17	27	**
SEE I/II	13	19	18
SER/JOBS I/II	10	**	14

**Samples were too small to report.
a. Job-search assistance was also received.

When interpreting these findings one should note that program enrollment periods represent the time elapsed between official enrollment and termination. Due to reporting lags and idiosyncratic record-keeping, enrollment periods probably overstate the amount of active time in the program and contain a large amount of random measurement error. Therefore, tables 5.9 and 5.10 provide only rough approximations of the time spent in each program.

NOTES

1. For applicants who only want immediate assistance in finding a job, and do not want to spend time in a retraining program, job-search assistance alone may be more attractive. On the other hand, a program which offers—but does not require—services like retraining will be more attractive than one with a less rich service mix.

2. This may be especially important for single parents.

3. The quasi-experimental component of the Buffalo demonstration (for nontarget plants) was used for this comparison because its participation rates were reported as a percentage of applicants. The Buffalo experimental component reported participation in a way that was not comparable to the present analysis.

4. The only OJT slots at TEC/HCC were for bus drivers at the local transportation authority.

5. The discussion that follows is in terms of mean enrollment durations. The same basic findings were reflected by median durations.

6
Treatment and Control
Group Experiences

This chapter lays the empirical groundwork for estimating program impacts on earnings, employment, and UI benefits by comparing these labor market outcomes for treatment and control group members.

Outcome Measures and Analysis Samples

Chapter 3 described the three sources of outcome data used for the analysis:

1. state UI wage records
2. a brief telephone follow-up survey
3. state UI benefit records

Table 6.1 lists the principal outcome measures constructed from each data source, plus their observation periods and analysis sample sizes.

The most important outcome measures used for the analysis were quarterly earnings and employment based on UI wage records. These records provided consistent information on total UI-covered earnings for three quarters before random assignment, the quarter in which random assignment occurred, and four quarters thereafter. Records were obtained for the 2,192-person experimental sample. The last 406 persons to be randomly assigned were deleted because their UI wage records at the time covered only three post-assignment quarters.[1] Seven additional persons were eliminated because their quarterly earnings were so high that data errors were suspected.[2] Consequently, the UI wage sample contained 1,779 persons.

The second outcome data source was a brief telephone survey conducted one year after random assignment. The 74-percent response rate for this survey yielded an analysis sample of 1,643 persons. Respondents were asked about the number of weeks they had worked during their third and fourth quarters after random assignment, and two outcome measures were constructed from their responses:

1. number of weeks worked
2. employment status

Table 6.1
Outcome Measures by Data Source

	Observation period	Sample size
UI wage records		1,779
Earnings	Quarters –3, –2, –1, 0, 1, 2,	
Employed or not	3, and 4 from random	
	assignment	
Follow-up survey		1,643
Weeks worked	Quarters 3 and 4 after	
Employed or not	random assignment	
Weekly earnings	One year after random	
Employed or not	assignment	
UI benefit records		2,192
Amount received	Weeks 0, 10, 20, and 30 after	
Received or not	random assignment	

Survey respondents also were asked if they were employed during the week they were interviewed. If employed, they were asked how much they had earned. Two outcome measures were constructed from these responses:

1. employment status one year after random assignment;
2. weekly earnings at the time, with zero earnings for persons not employed.

The third outcome data source was UI benefit records for the 2,192-person experimental sample. Individual benefit histories were examined to determine whether or not benefits had been received during weeks 10, 20, and 30 after random assignment. Total dollar benefits received during this period were also computed.

Different outcome data sources produced different analysis samples (table 6.2). UI benefit data produced the largest samples, comprising all 2,192 experimental sample members.[3] UI wage data produced the next largest samples, totaling 1,779 persons. Follow-up survey data produced the smallest samples, totaling 1,643 persons. These samples provide the basis for the treatment and control group comparisons presented in this chapter.[4]

Table 6.2
Analysis Sample Sizes
for Treatment and Control Group Outcome Comparisons

	UI wage sample	Survey sample	UI benefit sample
Men			
TEC/HCC	690	618	832
SEE	192	156	227
SER/JOBS	221	238	307
Women			
TEC/HCC	176	147	194
SEE	265	218	303
SER/JOBS	235	266	329
Total	1,779	1,643	2,192

Earnings Comparisons

Baseline Experiences

Figures 6.1–6.3 compare treatment and control group earnings for a three-quarter baseline period, the random assignment quarter, and a four-quarter follow-up period. First, consider the baseline period. Perhaps most striking is the precipitous earnings decline experienced by all groups. This *preprogram dip* is consistent with findings from prior research (Ashenfelter 1978; Kiefer 1979; Bassi 1984; Bloom 1984b; Bloom 1987b; Bryant and Rupp 1987; Dickinson, Johnson and West 1986). The central issue posed by this phenomenon is the extent to which it represents short-term unemployment versus permanent economic displacement.

Short-term unemployment reflects the considerable movement in and out of jobs that occurs in all labor markets. Because employment and training programs target persons who are out of work, or who have current incomes below a specified level, or both, they inevitably over-sample persons who have recently experienced a temporary job loss. Subsequent movement back toward prior earnings levels thus will occur, as these short-term setbacks are reversed.[5] However, this recovery may be slow and incomplete for sample members who have permanently lost jobs with no comparable replacements.

Consider the experience of control group members, which reflects what probably would have happened to treatment group members in the absence of the demonstration. First, note that control group earnings rose sharply after random assignment; hence, much of their preprogram dip was temporary. Nevertheless, peak control group follow-up earnings ranged from only 66 to 71 percent of baseline levels for men, and 61 to 78 percent for women. In other words, these groups did not fully regain their prior earnings power. This finding is consistent with the discussion in chapter 4, which indicated that sample members experienced serious economic displacement.

A second important baseline finding is that treatment and control group prior earnings were quite similar. This supports the conclusion in chapter 4 that treatment and control groups for the demonstration were suffi-

Figure 6.1
Mean Quarterly Earnings at TEC/HCC

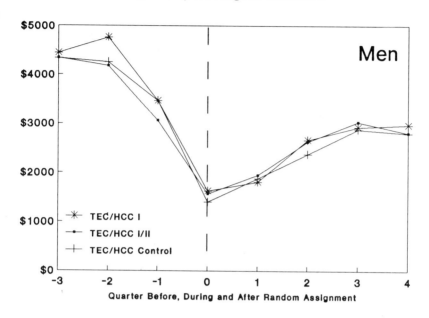

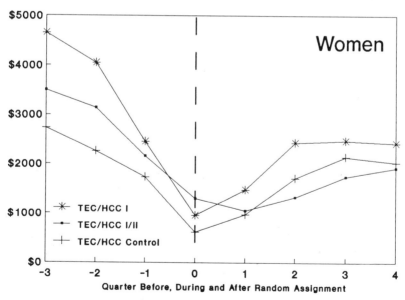

Figure 6.2
Mean Quarterly Earnings at SEE

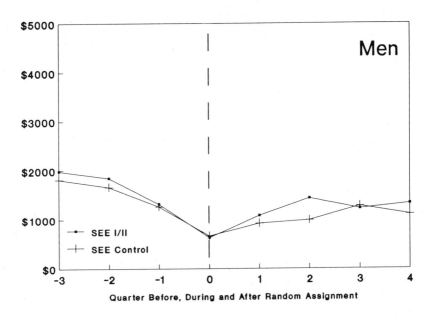

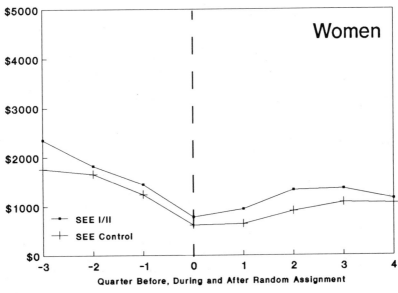

Figure 6.3
Mean Quarterly Earnings at SER/JOBS

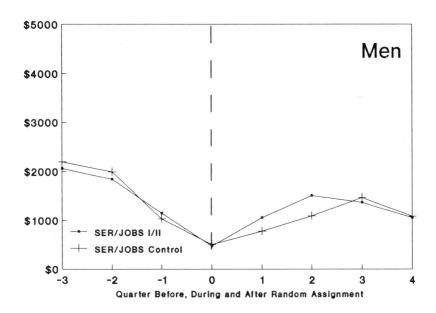

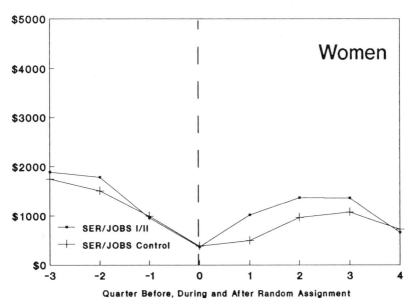

ciently comparable to provide valid program impact estimates. The only exception was TEC/HCC women, who were not included in the impact analysis because their samples were very small and not comparable.

A third key baseline finding is that TEC/HCC sample members earned more than twice as much as their SEE and SER/JOBS counterparts. This reflects the major differences between the Houston and El Paso economies discussed in chapter 1, as well as differences in site targeting strategies. A final baseline finding worthy of note is that men from all three sites earned far more than women. This outcome is consistent with virtually all prior related research and indeed, has Biblical antecedents.[6]

Follow-Up Experiences

Table 6.3 summarizes follow-up earnings experiences for all men in the sample and women from the El Paso sites.[7] First note that male treatment group members earned $103, $339, $26, and $81 more than controls during the first four quarters after random assignments. This represents differences of 8, 20, 1, and 4 percent, respectively. By the end of the first year after random assignment, during the week that sample members were interviewed for the follow-up survey, there was virtually no sign of a treatment group earnings advantage. Thus, male treatment group members experienced an early, brief, and modest earnings gain, which produced a $549, or 8 percent, treatment group advantage for the year.

Table 6.3
Treatment and Control Group Earnings Differences

	All men		El Paso women	
	Dollars	**Percent**	**Dollars**	**Percent**
1st UI quarter	103	8	404**	71**
2nd UI quarter	339*	20*	416**	45**
3rd UI quarter	26	1	288**	27**
4th UI quarter	81	4	21	2
Total	549	8	1,126**	32**
Survey week	−10	−4	18*	20*

* or **=statistically significant positive difference at the 0.05 or 0.01 level, one-tail.

Quarterly earnings gains for El Paso women were $404, $416, $288, and $21, or 71, 45, 27, and 2 percent, respectively; hence, during the first three follow-up quarters, women in the El Paso treatment groups earned far more than controls. Evidence for the fourth quarter is difficult to interpret, however, because of probable data reporting problems discussed in appendix 3.2. Nevertheless, survey responses indicate that the treatment group advantage was still observable during the interview week, one year after random assignment; hence, it probably persisted beyond the follow-up period. The total female treatment group advantage for the year after random assignment was $1,126, or 32 percent.

Employment Comparisons

Baseline Experiences

Figures 6.4–6.6 describe the employment experiences of treatment and control groups from each site, based on measures constructed from UI wage data. Specifically, the percentage of sample members who were employed each quarter was measured as the percentage with non-zero UI-reported earnings.

As can be seen, highest employment rates (ranging from 71 to 91 percent) were experienced during the earliest baseline quarter. This reflects the fact that prior employment was an eligibility requirement for the demonstration. Further evidence of the extensive prior employment of sample members is the fact that 86 to 95 percent had UI-reported earnings during *at least one* of their three baseline quarters.[8] However, all groups experienced a precipitous decline in employment prior to random assignment, which mirrored their *preprogram earnings dip.*

Follow-Up Experiences

Table 6.4 suggests that there was no treatment group employment advantage for men after random assignment. Treatment and control group employment rates were almost identical during all four UI follow-up quarters. Percent employed during both the survey week—one year after random assignment—and the third and fourth survey follow-up

Figure 6.4
Percent Employed by Quarter at TEC/HCC

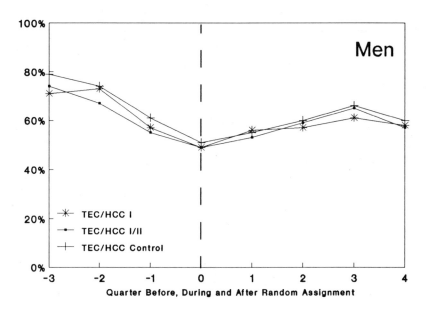

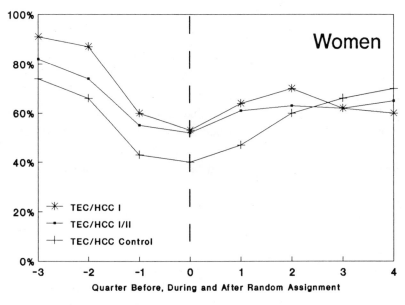

Figure 6.5
Percent Employed by Quarter at SEE

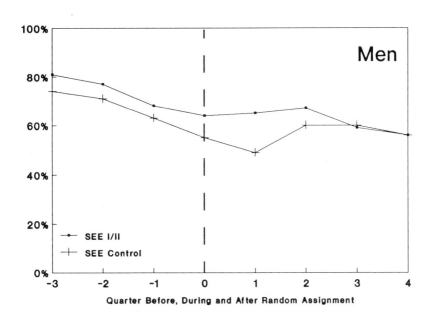

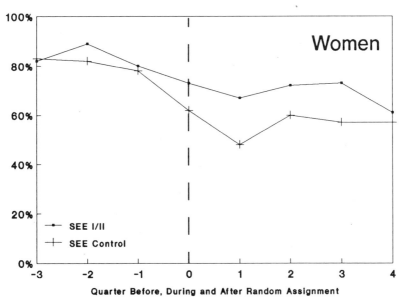

Figure 6.6
Percent Employed by Quarter at SER/JOBS

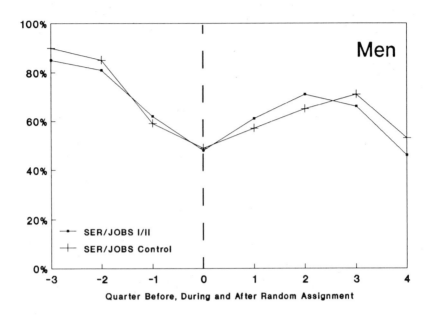

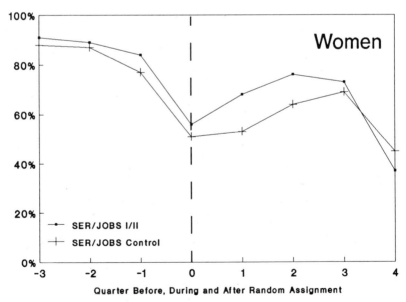

quarters were also virtually identical. In addition, weeks worked during this period were about the same.

This appears to conflict with the substantial second-quarter treatment group earnings advantage cited above. But it might simply reflect treatment group members who became reemployed earlier during this quarter than controls. If so, quarterly treatment group earnings could exceed that for controls, because treatment group members would have been employed longer, even if the percentage of both groups employed at the end of the quarter was the same.

Table 6.4
Treatment and Control Group
Employment Differences

	All men	El Paso women
Percent employed		
1st UI quarter	3	18**
2nd UI quarter	2	12**
3rd UI quarter	–3	10**
4th UI quarter	–3	–2
Weeks worked		
3rd survey quarter	0.7	1.4**
4th survey quarter	–0.1	0.9*
Percent employed		
3rd or 4th survey quarter	2	8*
Survey week	<1	6

* or **=statistically significant at the 0.05 or 0.01 level, one-tail.

In contrast, table 6.4 suggests a dramatic treatment group employment advantage for El Paso women. This advantage was substantial during the first three UI follow-up quarters, the third and fourth survey follow-up quarters, and the survey week, one year after random assignment.[9] Hence, employment experiences for women are consistent with their earnings histories and suggest a large, sustained treatment group advantage.

UI Benefit Comparisons

Baseline Experiences

Figures 6.7–6.9 illustrate the difference between UI benefit histories for treatment and control group members. The 30-week follow-up period for this comparison reflects the limited duration of UI benefit entitlements—26 weeks for regular benefits plus six to eight additional weeks for extended benefits. Because most sample members were receiving UI benefits when they applied to the program, those who remained unemployed exhausted their benefit entitlements soon thereafter. Thus, by the end of the 30-week period, there was little remaining margin for a treatment/control group difference.[10]

As can be seen, the overwhelming majority of sample members were receiving UI when they entered the demonstration. For men the rate was 84 percent at SER/JOBS, 69 percent at TEC/HCC, and 66 percent at SEE. For women it was 88 percent at SER/JOBS, 78 percent at SEE, and 67 percent at TEC/HCC. This reflects program decisions to recruit mainly UI claimants, both because they comprised a large available client pool, and because UI payments counted toward sites' resource matching requirements.

Table 6.5 indicates virtually no differences between treatment and control group UI benefit receipt rates at random assignment. This further supports the conclusion that treatment and control groups were sufficiently comparable to provide valid program impact estimates.

Follow-Up Experiences

Table 6.5 also suggests that both male and female treatment groups experienced a substantial UI benefit reduction, relative to controls. This occurred early and declined continually over time. On balance, male treatment group members received $174, or 14 percent, less than controls during their first 30 weeks after random assignment; female treatment group members received $152, or 14 percent, less.

Figure 6.7
Percent Receiving UI by Week After Random Assignment
at TEC/HCC

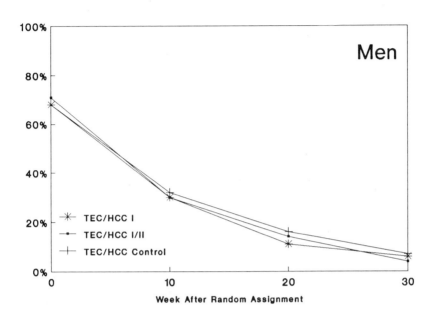

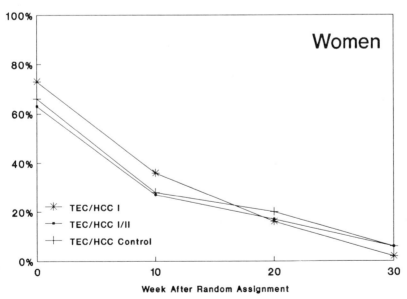

Figure 6.8
Percent Receiving UI by Week After Random Assignment
at SEE

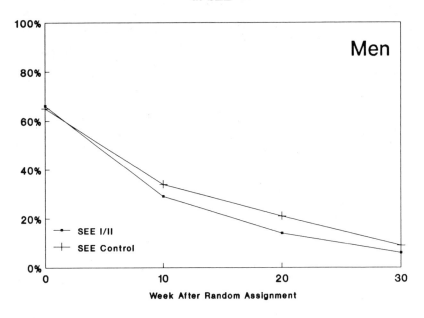

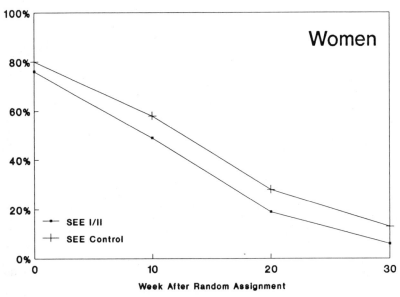

Figure 6.9
Percent Receiving UI by Week After Random Assignment
at SER/JOBS

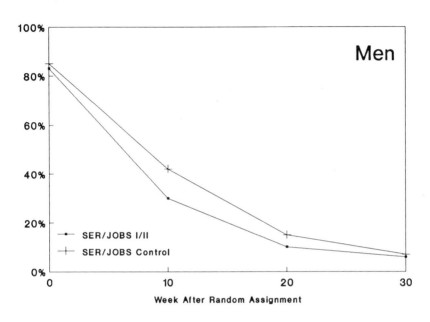

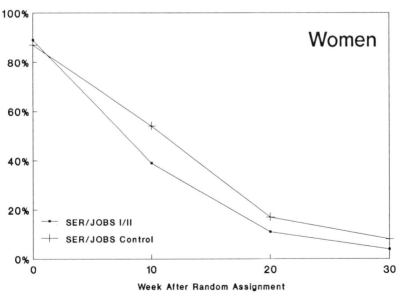

Table 6.5
Treatment and Control Group
UI Benefit Differences

	All men	El Paso women
Percent on UI		
Week 0	–2	–1
Week 10	–6**	–12**
Week 20	–4**	–8**
Week 30	–2	–6**
30-week benefits		
Dollars	–174**	–152**
Percent	–14**	–14**

** =statistically significant lower treatment group benefits at the 0.05 or 0.01 level, one-tail. No significant findings were only significant at the 0.05 level.

Summary

This chapter has described the baseline earnings, employment, and UI benefit experiences of treatment and control group members, and has identified key features of their corresponding follow-up experiences. The basic pattern that emerges is an early, small, temporary treatment group advantage for men and a much larger and more persistent treatment group advantage for women. These differences provide the basis for program impact estimates presented in the next chapter.

NOTES

1. Because random assignment was continuous over time, deleting the last 406 assignees did not affect the internal validity of the remaining sample. Sensitivity analyses indicate that impact findings for the first three post-assignment quarters were comparable when estimated with or without this group.
2. Their quarterly earnings exceeded $15,000.
3. If there was no record of a UI benefit payment to a sample member for a specific week, it was assumed that zero benefits had been paid, because benefit checks were computerized and their records were automated.
4. The next chapter presents program impact estimates based on regression-adjusted treatment and control group outcome comparisons. Its sample sizes were about 100 persons, or 5 percent, smaller in total because of missing data for some independent variables in the regression models used.

5. This phenomenon represents a statistical artifact called *regression to the mean* (Campbell 1975).

6. "When a man explicitly vows to the Lord the equivalent for a human being, the following scale shall apply: If it is a male from twenty to sixty years of age, the equivalent is fifty shekels of silver by the sanctuary weight; if it is a female, the equivalent is thirty shekels" (Leviticus 27:2-4).

7. These estimates were obtained from a regression for each follow-up quarter that specified earnings as the dependent variable, plus site-specific dummy variables, and a dummy variable to identify treatment group members, as its independent variables. The coefficient for the treatment dummy was reported as the treatment and control group difference in tables 6.3 to 6.5.

8. The remainder probably held jobs not covered by UI, or became unemployed before the baseline period.

9. Recall that fourth quarter UI follow-up data are probably subject to reporting errors.

10. This highlights an important issue that arises when using UI benefits to measure labor market success. One can reasonably assume that persons receiving unemployment insurance are unemployed. However, when one does not observe persons receiving benefits, it is not clear whether they are unemployed or have exhausted their benefits.

Appendix 6.1
Treatment and Control Group
Follow-Up Experiences by Site

This appendix supplements the discussion in chapter 6 by presenting tables that describe additional treatment and control group follow-up experiences by site (tables 6A1.1 – 6A1.4).

Table 6A1.1
Weekly Earnings One Year After Random Assignment
(Includes Zero Earnings)

		Men	Women
TEC/HCC	I	403	226
	I/II	339	217
	Control	370	167
SEE	I/II	134	121
	Control	144	105
SER/JOBS	I/II	137	104*
	Control	157	84

*=statistically significant treatment group advantage at the 0.05 level, one-tail. No treatment group advantage was significant at the 0.01 level.

Table 6A1.2
Employment Experience from Follow-Up Survey
(Men)

		Mean weeks worked		Percent employed	
		3rd follow-up quarter	4th follow-up quarter	3rd or 4th follow-up quarter	Survey week
TEC/HCC	I	10.2	10.5	93**	82
	I/II	9.2	9.9	85	74
	Control	8.9	9.8	84	75
SEE	I/II	7.5	8.4	80	66
	Control	6.8	8.2	74	67
SER/JOBS	I/II	8.6	8.0	84	71
	Control	7.9	9.1	88	74

**=statistically significant treatment group advantage at the 0.01 level, one-tail. No significant finding was only significant at the 0.05 level.

127

Table 6A1.3
Employment Experience from Follow-Up Survey
(Women)

		Mean weeks worked		Percent employed	
		3rd follow-up quarter	4th follow-up quarter	3rd or 4th follow-up quarter	Survey week
TEC/HCC I		9.6	9.6	84	68
	I/II	7.7	8.7	79	73
	Control	8.6	7.8	81	65
SEE	I/II	8.4*	9.1*	84*	69
	Control	6.8	7.9	72	68
SER/JOBS I/II		8.2*	8.0	80	68*
	Control	7.0	7.3	75	58

*=statistically significant lower treatment group benefits at the 0.05 level, one-tail. No treatment group benefit reduction was significant at the 0.01 level.

Table 6A1.4
30-Week UI Benefits
(Dollars)

		Men	Women
TEC/HCC I		1,311	1,316
	I/II	1,294	1,321
	Control	1,462	1,208
SEE	I/II	894	1,153
	Control	1,049	1,279
SER/JOBS I/II		867*	816**
	Control	1,081	991

* or **=statistically significant lower treatment group benefits at the 0.05 or 0.01 level, one-tail.

Appendix 6.2
Survey Versus UI Employment Findings
for TEC/HCC I Men

The only major inconsistency between follow-up findings from different data sources occurred for TEC/HCC I men. UI data for this group indicate post-assignment earnings gains that were small and short-lived; whereas, survey data suggest larger and longer-lasting gains. Table 6A2.1 provides insight into this problem by comparing UI and survey employment measures for the third post-assignment follow-up quarter.[1] Fourth follow-up quarter findings were not used because of probable UI data reporting problems identified in appendix 3.2.

Table 6A2.1
Percent Employed During Third Follow-Up Quarter
for Subsample with UI and Survey Data

	UI data	Survey data
TEC/HCC I	64	87
Control	69	71

UI employment measures for table 6A2.1 were constructed by counting any sample member with reported earnings during a quarter as employed. Survey employment measures were constructed by counting any respondent who reported weeks worked during a quarter as employed. These measures were reported for the subsample with both available. As can be seen, survey responses indicate that TEC/HCC I men were far more likely than controls to be employed, whereas UI data suggest no such treatment group advantage.

One explanation for this discrepancy is that TEC/HCC I men may have pursued self-employment to a greater extent than controls. Self-employment was promoted by Career Circles during Tier I as a viable route to reemployment. But self-employment earnings were not covered by UI in Texas at the time; thus, self-employment earnings were not reported by UI wage records.

NOTE

1. Recall that survey follow-up quarters are four to five weeks earlier than follow-up quarters for UI employment measures (appendix 3.2).

7
Program Impacts

This chapter examines program impacts on earnings, employment, and UI benefits. It first summarizes the effects of being offered program services—referred to as *treatment group impacts*. It next summarizes the effects of receiving program services—referred to as *participant impacts*. It then compares impacts for Tier I Only versus Tier I/II program strategies. Finally, it explores differences in impacts for participant subgroups.

Treatment Group Impacts
The Effect of Being Offered Program Services

Estimation Procedure

Chapter 2 briefly described how the effects of being offered program services were estimated from regression-adjusted treatment and control group outcome comparisons. Impacts on continuous outcomes (earnings and total UI benefits) were estimated using ordinary least squares regressions. Impacts on discrete outcomes (employment and UI benefit receipt rates) were estimated using maximum likelihood LOGIT models (Pindyck and Rubinfeld 1976; Borsch-Supan 1987).[1]

Table 7.1 summarizes the independent variables in the impact estimation models. The first variables listed are individual background characteristics. Four of these characteristics—age, education, ethnicity, and prior occupation—were represented by a set of dummy (1/0) variables, with an omitted baseline category.[2] These variables represent standard human capital measures used to control for individual labor market prospects. The fifth individual characteristic—random assignment week—was represented by the week (1–13) during the UI quarter in which random assignment occurred. This variable was included to account for individual differences in the timing of UI follow-up quarters.

Table 7.1
Impact Estimation Model

Dependent variable[a]	
Y	earnings, employment, or UI benefits

Background characteristics[b]	
AGE35–44	1 if 35–44; 0 otherwise
AGE45–54	1 if 45–54; 0 otherwise
AGE55+	1 if 55+; 0 otherwise
ED12	1 if high school degree only; 0 otherwise
ED>12	1 if beyond high school degree; 0 otherwise
BLACK	1 if Black, non-Hispanic; 0 otherwise
HISPANIC	1 if Hispanic; 0 otherwise
WHITECOL	1 if laid-off white-collar worker; 0 otherwise
BLUECOL	1 if laid-off blue-collar worker; 0 otherwise
RAWEEK	Week randomly assigned during assignment quarter (1–13)

Prior earnings, employment, or UI status[b]	
EARN(–1)	UI-reported earnings in the 1st, 2nd, and 3rd quarters
EARN(–2)	before random assignment. Used for UI earnings, and all
EARN(–3)	survey outcome regressions
EMP(–1)	Employed (1) or not (0), according to UI data for the 1st,
EMP(–2)	2nd, and 3rd quarters before random assignment. Used
EMP(–3)	for UI employment outcome regressions
UI(–10)	Receiving UI (1) or not (0) 10 weeks before random assignment
UI(0)	Receiving UI (1) or not (0) at random assignment

Site Indicators[b]	
SEE	1 if SEE; 0 otherwise
SER/JOBS	1 if SER/JOBS; 0 otherwise

Treatment group indicator	
TREATMENT	1 if treatment group member; 0 otherwise

a. OLS regressions were used for impacts on continuous outcomes, and maximum likelihood LOGIT models were used for impacts on discrete outcomes.
b. All categorical independent variables had omitted baseline categories.

The second set of independent variables in the table represent prior earnings, employment, and UI status. These lagged outcome variables help to control for all measured and unmeasured factors that determine future labor market potential. The third set of independent variables are site indicators, which control for unmeasured site differences in sample backgrounds and labor market conditions.[3]

The last independent variable distinguishes treatment group members from controls. Its coefficient represents the average treatment group impact for the sample from which the regression was estimated. To summarize treatment group impacts, they were pooled (averaged) for men from all three sites and for women from El Paso. This was done by estimating separate regressions for all men and for El Paso women. Houston women were not included because, as indicated in chapter 4, their small treatment and control groups were not sufficiently comparable to provide valid impact estimates.

As a further guide to interpreting findings reported in this chapter, appendix 7.1 presents their site-specific counterparts. In general these findings were consistent with the average estimates presented below.

One last point to note when interpreting program impact findings concerns their statistical significance. Statistical significance is a reflection of the probability that a sample-based finding represents a true finding for the population from which the sample was drawn, instead of a chance event due to sampling error. Statistical significance does not necessarily indicate whether a finding is large, policy-relevant, or substantively important; rather, it provides a guide for how confident one should be that a finding is real. One should place more confidence in findings that are statistically significant, according to commonly accepted criteria, than in findings that are not.

Treatment Group Impacts for Men

Tables 7.2–7.4 summarize average treatment group impacts on earnings, employment, and UI benefits.

Table 7.2
Treatment Group Earnings Impacts

	All men		El Paso women	
	Dollars	**Percent**	**Dollars**	**Percent**
1st UI quarter	73	5	413**	69**
2nd UI quarter	329*	16*	371**	38**
3rd UI quarter	3	<1	248**	22**
4th UI quarter	66	3	−45	−5
Total	471	5	987**	28**
Survey week	−7	−2	15*	16*

* or **=statistically significant at the 0.05 or 0.01 level, one-tail.

Table 7.3
Treatment Group Employment Impacts

	All men	El Paso women
Percent employed		
1st UI quarter	2	20**
2nd UI quarter	3	12**
3rd UI quarter	−3	10**
4th UI quarter	−3	−3
Weeks worked		
3rd survey quarter	0.9**	1.5**
4th survey quarter	0.2	0.9*
Percent employed		
3rd or 4th survey quarter	4	9**
Survey week	1	6

* or **=statistically significant at the 0.05 or 0.01 level, one-tail.

Table 7.4
Treatment Group UI Impacts

	All men	El Paso women
Percent on UI		
Week 10	–6*	–17**
Week 20	–3	–9**
Week 30	–1	–6**
30-week benefits		
Dollars	–143*	–193**
Percent	–11*	–17**

* or ** = statistically significant at the 0.05 or 0.01 level, one-tail.

With respect to impacts on *earnings*:

UI wage data indicated that male treatment group members experienced moderate program-induced earnings gains during their second follow-up quarter. These gains averaged $329, or 16 percent, and were statistically significant. Negligible subsequent gains were experienced; hence, total impacts for the first year after random assignment averaged $471, or 5 percent, which was not statistically significant.

With respect to impacts on *employment*:

UI records suggested no large or statistically significant effects. However, follow-up survey data indicated that time employed during the third follow-up quarter was increased by a statistically significant 0.9 weeks. Thereafter, neither data source indicated an employment effect.

With respect to impacts on *UI benefits*:

All male treatment groups experienced a program-induced reduction in UI benefit receipt rates, which occurred soon after random assignment and diminished continually thereafter. The corresponding 30-week benefit reduction averaged a statistically significant $143, or 11 percent.

In summary, it appears that men who were offered Worker Adjustment Demonstration services experienced modest and brief program-induced earnings gains and substantial UI benefit reductions.

Treatment Group Impacts for El Paso Women

Treatment group impacts for El Paso women occurred sooner, were larger, and lasted longer than those for men.

With respect to impacts on *earnings*:

UI data indicated large program-induced earnings gains during each of the first three follow-up quarters. These impacts were statistically significant and averaged $413, or 69 percent; $371, or 38 percent; and $248, or 22 percent. Fourth-quarter results are difficult to interpret because of probable data reporting problems (appendix 3.2). In total, earnings gains for the first follow-up year averaged $987, or 28 percent, and were statistically significant. Furthermore, at the end of this year, during the follow-up survey week, there was a $15, or 16 percent, treatment group earnings advantage. Hence, earnings gains for El Paso women probably continued beyond the one-year follow-up period for the present study.

With respect to impacts on *employment*:

UI data suggested a statistically significant 20, 12, and 10 percentage point increase in the likelihood of employment during the first three follow-up quarters.[4] Likewise, survey data indicated that the program increased average time worked by 1.5 weeks and 0.9 weeks during the third and fourth follow-up quarters. Survey data also indicated that the likelihood of employment anytime during this period was increased by 9 percentage points, and the likelihood of employment one year after random assignment, during the survey week, was increased by 6 percentage points. All but the last of these findings were statistically significant.

With respect to impacts on *UI benefits*:

The program reduced benefit receipt rates substantially for women. These reductions were statistically significant and averaged 17, 9, and 6 percentage points during follow-up weeks 10, 20, and 30. The corresponding average reduction in total benefit payments was a statistically significant $193, or 17 percent.

In summary, treatment group findings for women from El Paso indicated pronounced early impacts that diminished over time, but persisted for at least one year after random assignment, and probably longer.

Tier I Versus Tier I/II Treatment Group Impacts

One goal of the Worker Adjustment Demonstration was to compare the cost-effectiveness of two different approaches to helping displaced workers. The first approach—Tier I Only—focused exclusively on reemployment through job-search assistance. The second approach—Tier I/II—provided job-search assistance for all participants, followed by occupational skills training for some. Theory suggests greater impacts from the second approach—other things being equal—because it increases human capital and facilitates job search. This approach, however, is more costly and thus requires a greater return.

The basis for comparing Tier I Only with Tier I/II impacts is the experience of men from TEC/HCC, because this site randomly assigned eligible applicants to three experimental groups: Tier I Only, Tier I/II, and control status. Tier I Only net treatment group impacts were estimated from regression-adjusted comparisons of Tier I Only versus control group outcomes. Tier I/II net treatment group impacts were estimated from regression-adjusted Tier I/II versus control group outcome comparisons.

When comparing Tier I Only and Tier I/II net treatment group impacts, one should note that they reflect similar participation rates (62 percent for TEC/HCC I and 65 percent for TEC/HCC I/II). But TEC/HCC I participants received only job-search assistance; whereas, 37 percent of TEC/HCC I/II participants received some classroom training and 7 percent received OJT.

Table 7.5 suggests that essentially no additional gains accrued from adding Tier II services to job-search assistance. If anything, the Tier I treatment group seemed to experience slightly larger program impacts: $403 versus $320 earnings gains during the first year after random assignment; a 3.0 versus 0.9 week employment increase during the third and fourth follow-up quarters; and $145 versus $119 average UI benefit reductions during the first 30 weeks after random assignment.[5]

Table 7.5
Tier I Vs. Tier I/II Treatment Group Impacts
(Houston Men Only)

Impact	TEC/HCC I	TEC/HCC I/II
Earnings (Dollars)		
3rd follow-up quarter	57	120
4th follow-up quarter	147	–23
First follow-up year	403	320
Survey week	36	–21
Weeks worked		
3rd follow-up quarter	1.7**	0.4
4th follow-up quarter	1.3**	0.4
Total	3.0**	0.9[a]
30-week UI benefits		
Dollars	–145	–119

** =statistically significant at the 0.01 level, one-tail. No significant findings were significant at only the 0.05 level.
a. Components do not sum to exact total due to rounding.

When comparing Tier I Only and Tier I/II impacts, it is important to distinguish between in-program and postprogram findings. For example, classroom training—the main TEC/HCC II activity—may reduce in-program earnings, as participants attend class and are not available for jobs. OJT—an infrequent TEC/HCC II activity—may increase in-program earnings, through the subsidized employment it provides. The postprogram effects of these activities may be very different, however.

As a rough approximation, consider the postprogram period as starting when 90 percent of the treatment group were not enrolled in the program. This point was reached at 17 weeks into the UI follow-up period for TEC/HCC I men, and 23 weeks for TEC/HCC I/II men;[6]

hence, the third and fourth follow-up quarters represent postprogram outcomes for these groups. Table 7.5 indicates, however, that even during the *postprogram period,* Tier I/II did not outperform Tier I Only. Both groups experienced negligible postprogram earnings effects and Tier I Only reported larger impacts on weeks worked. The longest term postprogram impact measure available was earnings during the follow-up survey week, one year after random assignment. Even this measure did not suggest a larger Tier I/II effect.

When attempting to generalize the preceding finding it is important to recognize the conditions it represents. Recall that Houston Tier II occupational training was not well-matched to its participants. Specifically, the blue-collar HCC Tier II program was inconsistent with the backgrounds of its mostly white-collar TEC/HCC clients. Hence, TEC/HCC findings do not prove that supplementing job-search assistance with occupational training cannot be an effective strategy. Rather, they indicate that such an approach was not effective at TEC/HCC, given the mismatch between its Tier II program offerings and participants' backgrounds.

Participant Impacts
The Effect of Receiving Program Services

Displaced worker programs cannot mandate participation, they can only offer services. Thus, it is perhaps most relevant from a program's perspective to determine the impacts it can produce by making services available. From an applicant's perspective, however, it is most important to know what the likely impacts will be if he or she decides to participate.

To address this latter issue, it is necessary to first examine the relationship between treatment group impacts and participant impacts. In particular, it is important to understand how treatment group impacts reflect two factors:

1. The percentage of treatment group members who participate
2. The average impact for each participant

If all treatment group members participate, then impacts-per-treatment-group-member will equal impacts-per-participant, but if half of the treatment group participates, impacts-per-treatment-group-member will be half of the average impact-per-participant. This relationship reflects the fact that impacts-per-treatment-group-member allocate total impacts to all treatment group members (participants and no-shows); whereas, impacts-per-participant allocate this total to participants only.

Consider a 10-person treatment group with five participants and five no-shows. Assume a $1,000 earnings impact for each participant and zero impact for each no-show. The total impact for the group is $5,000. The average treatment group impact is therefore $5,000/10 or $500. The average participant impact is $5,000/5 or $1,000. More generally, to convert treatment group impacts to participant impacts, one need only divide the former by the participation rate, expressed as a proportion (Bloom 1984a). In the present example, this implies dividing the $500 treatment group impact by 0.5, which yields $500/0.5 or $1,000.

Impacts for Male and Female Participants

Tables 7.6 to 7.8 report average participant impacts for all men and El Paso women. These estimates were based on the treatment group impacts reported in tables 7.2 to 7.4 and their corresponding participation rates.

Table 7.6 illustrates the striking difference between earnings impacts for male and female participants. Male participants experienced a one-time, program-induced earnings gain during their second follow-up quarter. Female participants experienced consistently large, although declining, earnings gains during each of their first three follow-up quarters.

Overall, during the first year after random assignment, male participants experienced a $673 (8 percent) program-induced earnings gain. This impact, although substantial, was not statistically significant. The corresponding impact for women, however, was almost twice as large ($1,148, or 34 percent) and highly statistically significant. Furthermore, the earnings impact for women was still large ($17 weekly, or 19 percent) at the end of the one-year follow-up period, but for men it had long since disappeared.

Table 7.6
Earnings Impacts for Participants

	All men		El Paso women	
	Dollars	**Percent**	**Dollars**	**Percent**
1st UI quarter	104	7	480**	93**
2nd UI quarter	470*	26*	431**	45**
3rd UI quarter	4	<1	288**	28**
4th UI quarter	94	4	–52	–6
Total	673	8	1,148**	34**
Survey week	–10	–4	17*	19*

* or ** = statistically significant at the 0.05 or 0.01 level, one-tail.

Employment impacts for female participants (table 7.7) were consistent with their earnings impacts. Both UI and follow-up survey data indicate large gains that gradually diminished over time, but remained for at least one year after random assignment.

Table 7.7
Employment Impacts for Participants

	All men	El Paso women
Percent employed		
1st UI quarter	3	23**
2nd UI quarter	4	14**
3rd UI quarter	–5	12**
4th UI quarter	–5	–3
Weeks worked		
3rd survey quarter	1.3**	1.8**
4th survey quarter	0.3	1.1*
Percent employed		
3rd or 4th survey quarter	5	11**
Survey week	1	7

* or ** = statistically significant at the 0.05 or 0.01 level, one-tail.

For male participants the employment story was more complex. UI data indicate no employment effect, even during the second follow-up quarter, when substantial earnings gains were experienced. This may reflect a situation whereby male participants were reemployed earlier in the second follow-up quarter, but controls caught up by the end of the quarter. Hence, participants may have been employed longer and thereby earned more, but this difference did not persist.[7]

Table 7.8
UI Impacts for Participants

	All men	El Paso women
Percent on UI		
Week 10	–8*	–20**
Week 20	–5	–10**
Week 30	–1	–7**
30-week benefits		
Dollars	–207*	–227**
Percent	–13*	–19**

* or **=statistically significant at the 0.05 or 0.01 level, one-tail.

Last, note the participant impacts on UI benefit payments (table 7.8). These findings suggest appreciable, consistent but declining benefit reductions for men and women. Overall, male participants experienced a $207 (13 percent) benefit reduction and female participants experienced a $227 (19 percent) reduction. Findings for both groups were statistically significant.

Impacts for Selected Participant Subgroups

The final section of this chapter briefly examines Worker Adjustment Demonstration impacts on selected participant subgroups. The goal of this *exploratory* analysis is to generate hypotheses that might serve as a basis for future theories about how program impacts are achieved, for whom they are possible, and under what conditions they can be attained. The analysis was based on findings for three pooled samples:

1. the Houston male sample
2. the El Paso male sample
3. the El Paso female sample

To explore how impacts varied by type of participant within each pooled sample, subgroups were constructed on the following basis:

1. education
2. age
3. prior occupation
4. prior wage rate
5. prior job length
6. duration of unemployment

Treatment group impacts were estimated separately for each subgroup using the statistical model summarized in table 7.1. Participant impacts then were estimated by dividing treatment group impacts by corresponding participation rates. Subgroups were constructed in the following manner.

1. Each pooled sample was split into high school graduate and school dropout subsamples to represent education differences.
2. Age groups were defined as persons under 35 and 35 or older to reflect the approximate sample midpoint and thus produce roughly equal-sized subgroups.[8]
3. Occupational subgroups were defined in terms of white-collar versus blue-collar workers. Subsamples for other occupational groups were too small for analysis.
4. Prior wage subgroups were defined in terms of the median value for each pooled sample. *Low wages* were defined as those equal to or below the pooled sample median. *High wages* were defined as those above the median. This was done to ensure equal-sized analysis samples, although it implied a different wage rate for splitting each pooled sample ($12.82 for Houston men, $5.00 for El Paso men, and $4.49 for El Paso women). Thus, one can inter-

pret impact findings for low prior-wage individuals as those for the lower half of each sample, and impacts for high prior-wage persons as those for the upper half. However, one can only make general comparisons across samples.

5. Each pooled sample was also split into subgroups according to the duration of prior jobs. Pooled sample medians (1.6 years for Houston men, 1.5 years for El Paso men, and 3.2 years for El Paso women) were used to define *short* versus *long* prior jobs. This produced equal-sized subsamples, but implied different subgroup definitions for each sample.

6. Subgroups were defined in terms of how long sample members had been unemployed when they applied to the demonstration program. A direct measure was not available, so the following approximation was used: individuals with no UI-reported earnings in the quarter before random assignment were defined as the *lengthy unemployment* subgroup; individuals with some earnings were defined as the *brief unemployment* subgroup.[9]

Tables 7.9 through 7.11 summarize the results of this analysis. Sample sizes for each subgroup are listed in appendix 7.3.[10] First, consider the findings for Houston men. When doing so, recall that the first and most intensive portion of this program (at Career Circles) was located in an exclusive shopping mall, made extensive use of sophisticated paper and pencil exercises, and emphasized self-employment. In short, it was oriented toward better-educated white-collar professionals. Furthermore, this program activity was carefully designed and well-organized. Thus, it should provide a strong test of how much difference a job-search assistance program can make for laid-off workers at the higher end of the education, occupation, earnings, and experience distributions. Correspondingly, one might expect less benefits for individuals at the lower end of these distributions.

Table 7.9 suggests that this pattern of impacts indeed occurred. Far greater benefits were experienced by high school graduates, white-collar workers, more highly-paid workers, and workers with longer prior jobs. In contrast, reemployment for high school dropouts, blue-collar workers, and persons with short prior jobs may actually have been impeded by the program.[11] Because many findings in the table are not statistically significant, however, they should be viewed with caution; nevertheless, the overall pattern of findings is quite plausible.

Table 7.9
Subgroup Impacts for Houston Male Participants

| | | Impact | |
| | | | |
Subgroup	Earnings	Weeks worked	UI benefits
Dropout	–8,158*	–10.6	1,212*
HS graduate	911	3.7**	–295*
Under 35	–157	0.8	–93
35 plus	737	3.5*	–272
Blue-collar	–1,774	4.1	–143
White-collar	1,297	1.9	–168
Low prior wage	468	1.9	34
High prior wage	199	7.2**	–479*
Short prior job	–1,430	–0.7	–105
Long prior job	2,629	–10.1**	–448
Brief unemployment	973	4.5**	–359*
Lengthy unemployment	267	0.6	116

* or ** = statistically significant at the 0.05 or 0.01 level, one-tail.

Now consider findings for El Paso male participants. Recall that both El Paso programs were fairly general and basic in scope; hence, there is no reason to expect pronounced variations in subgroup impacts. Correspondingly, table 7.10 suggests no consistently large subgroup impact differences.

Last, consider the subgroup impacts for El Paso female participants (table 7.11). Although major subgroup differences existed, no clear pattern emerged. The most pronounced and consistent differences were in terms of age and length of prior job. Younger sample members, who had shorter tenure in prior jobs, experienced larger impacts. This might reflect their greater job mobility and, hence, their greater ability to use newly-learned job-search skills.

Table 7.10
Subgroup Impacts for El Paso Male Participants

		Impact	
Subgroup	Earnings	Weeks worked	UI benefits
Dropout	884	0.3	–21
HS graduate	274	0.1	–540**
Under 35	667	–0.2	–252*
35 plus	716	0.3	–239
Blue-collar	577	–0.5	–256*
White-collar	949	4.2	–375
Low prior wage	1,009*	0.7	–84
High prior wage	–545	–1.3	–241
Short prior job	487	–0.2	–143
Long prior job	637	1.0	–221
Brief unemployment	1,067	0.1	–268*
Lengthy unemployment	233	–0.2	–233*

* or ** = statistically significant at the 0.05 or 0.01 level, one-tail.

But why does this result differ from that for El Paso men? Perhaps it is because the long prior job category comprised longer jobs in El Paso for women (3.2 years and longer) than for men (1.5 years and longer). Hence, the inertia from holding a prior job may have been greater for women.

Further confusing the interpretation of female subgroup impacts is the fact that women who were unemployed longer experienced larger program impacts. Perhaps this reflected the fact that women who were

unemployed longer were less likely to expect being recalled to their
prior jobs, and hence, participated more actively in the program. If this
is the case, however, why did it not seem to occur for men?

Table 7.11
Subgroup Impacts for El Paso Female Participants

| | | Impact | |
Subgroup	Earnings	Weeks worked	UI benefits
Dropout	1,043**	1.5	−225**
HS graduate	1,402*	5.3**	−226
Under 35	1,647**	4.6**	−355**
35 plus	510	0.8	−82
Blue-collar	1,195**	2.5*	−267**
White-collar	969	4.6	−67
Low prior wage	1,108**	1.6	−227**
High prior wage	851	2.4	−225*
Short prior job	1,081*	3.0*	−310**
Long prior job	729	0.4	14
Brief unemployment	831*	1.9	−221**
Lengthy unemployment	1,731*	4.6*	−238

* or **=statistically significant at the 0.05 or 0.01 level, one-tail.

On balance, however, the main conclusion to be drawn from the
preceding subgroup analysis is that *a program designed for better-
educated, more highly-paid white-collar workers can be effective for
this group, but such a program may be counterproductive for participants
with more limited education and job-skills.* A second major conclusion
suggests that *education, age, prior occupation, prior wage rate, prior
job length, and unemployment duration have no single pattern of influence on program effectiveness. Their roles vary substantially across
different programs and target groups.*

NOTES

1. Logistic regressions (LOGIT models) specify the dependent variable as the natural logarithm of the odds (Pindyck and Rubinfeld 1976). Coefficients for each independent variable, therefore, represent the rate of change in log-odds per unit change in the independent variable. These coefficients can readily be converted to the change in probability per unit change in the independent variable (Pindyck and Rubinfeld 1976).

2. In a regression with an intercept term, if one uses dummy (1/0) variables to represent mutually exclusive, collectively exhaustive categories of a single dimension (e.g., age), one must omit a category. Not omitting this *baseline category,* will cause the set of dummy variables to be perfectly collinear with the intercept term and prevent the regression from being estimated.

3. TEC/HCC was the omitted baseline site.

4. Once again, UI fourth follow-up quarter results are difficult to interpret because of data reporting problems (appendix 3.2).

5. One potential complication for comparisons of TEC/HCC I and TEC/HCC I/II net impacts is the fact that layoff job wages appear to be higher for TEC/HCC I (table 4.5). Appendix 7.2 demonstrates that this probably does not affect the conclusions of the analysis, however.

6. Ninety percent of the treatment group were not enrolled for men in SEE I/II, and SER/JOBS I/II at 20 and 12 weeks into the UI follow-up period, respectively. For SEE I/II and SER/JOBS I/II women, this point was reached at follow-up weeks 22 and 11.

7. This situation was identified in chapter 6.

8. Median age was 38 for Houston men, 33 for El Paso men, and 35 for El Paso women.

9. As an alternative, the *lengthy unemployment* subgroup was defined to include all persons who were not employed during *both* of the first two baseline quarters. Sample sizes for this group were too small for analysis, however.

10. Subgroup sample sizes do not add to the same total because of different numbers of missing observations for different variables used to define subgroups.

11. The extreme negative impacts for Houston male high school dropouts were based on very small samples, ranging from 30 to 54 persons. The negative impact for blue-collar workers, however, was based on 252 sample members, and the negative impact for persons with short prior jobs was based on a sample of 212.

Appendix 7.1
Treatment Group Impact Estimates by Site

Tables 7A1.1–7A1.6 present treatment group impacts for men and women by site. These impact estimates were obtained from regression and LOGIT models of the form described in table 7.1, by replacing the single treatment group variable, TREATMENT, with four site-specific treatment group variables:

HCCTEC1 = 1 if HCC/TEC I; 0 otherwise
HCCTEC12 = 1 if HCC/TEC I/II; 0 otherwise
SEE12 = 1 if SEE I/II; 0 otherwise
SER/JOBS12 = 1 if SER/JOBS I/II; 0 otherwise

Separate models were estimated for men and for women. Men from all sites and women from the two El Paso sites were included in the analysis.

Table 7A1.1
Male Treatment Group Earnings Impacts by Site
(dollars)

	TEC/HCC I	TEC/HCC I/II	SEE I/II	SER/JOBS I/II
1st UI quarter	−74	−13	135	321
2nd UI quarter	273	236	421	461
3rd UI quarter	57	120	−254	−41
4th UI quarter	147	−23	208	−1
Total	403	320	509	739
Survey week	36	−21	−12	−22

NOTE: No findings were statistically significant at the 0.05 level, one-tail.

149

Table 7A1.2
Male Treatment Group Employment Impacts by Site

	TEC/HCC I	TEC/HCC I/II	SEE I/II	SER/JOBS I/II
Percent employed				
1st UI quarter	<1	−1	11	3
2nd UI quarter	−3	<1	8	10
3rd UI quarter	−4	−1	−6	−3
4th UI quarter	−2	−3	<1	−7
Weeks worked				
3rd survey quarter	1.7**	0.4	0.7	0.9
4th survey quarter	1.3**	0.4	0.3	−0.9
Percent employed				
3rd or 4th survey quarter	10**	1	11	−1
Survey week	7	<1	−1	−2

**=statistically significant at the 0.01 level, one-tail. No significant findings were only significant at the 0.05 level.

Table 7A1.3
Male Treatment Group UI Benefit Impacts by Site

	TEC/HCC I	TEC/HCC I/II	SEE I/II	SER/JOBS I/II
Percent on UI				
Week 10	−3	−2	−6	−12*
Week 20	−6*	<1	−5	−3
Week 30	<1	−2	−3	2
30-week benefits ($)	−145	−119	−185	−142

*=statistically significant at the 0.05 level, one-tail. No findings were significant at the 0.01 level.

Table 7A1.4
El Paso Female Treatment Group Earnings Impacts by Site

	SEE I/II	SER/JOBS I/II
1st UI quarter	302*	508**
2nd UI quarter	351*	376*
3rd UI quarter	204	278
4th UI quarter	–30	–77
Total	827	1,086*
Survey week	4	20

* or **=statistically significant at the 0.05 or 0.01 level, one-tail.

Table 7A1.5
El Paso Female Treatment Group Employment Impacts by Site

	SEE I/II	SER/JOBS I/II
Percent employed		
1st UI quarter	23**	16**
2nd UI quarter	11*	11*
3rd UI quarter	17**	3
4th UI quarter	<1	–8
Weeks worked		
3rd survey quarter	1.6*	1.4*
4th survey quarter	1.0	0.8
Percent employed		
3rd or 4th survey quarter	12*	7
Survey week	–3	12*

* or **=statistically significant at the 0.05 or 0.01 level, one-tail.

Table 7A1.6
El Paso Female Treatment Group UI Benefit Impacts by Site

	SEE I/II	SER/JOBS I/II
Percent on UI		
Week 10	–12*	–17**
Week 20	–9	–8*
Week 30	–7*	–4*
30-week benefits ($)	–126	–212**

* or **=statistically significant at the 0.05 or 0.01 level, one-tail.

Appendix 7.2
Controlling for Layoff-Job Wage Rates
in Treatment Group Impact Estimates

Table 4.6 suggests that wage rates for men in their layoff jobs were statistically significantly higher for TEC/HCC I than for TEC/HCC I/II ($14.48 versus $13.12). It was important, therefore, to consider how this difference might affect Tier I versus Tier I/II impact comparisons.

The first point to recognize is that layoff job wage differences in table 4.6 are based on data for only a fraction of the sample—70 percent for TEC/HCC I men and 69 percent for TEC/HCC I/II men. Hence, there may be little difference for the full sample upon which impact estimates were based. Instead, the observed difference may reflect differences in missing data patterns for layoff-job wage rates. To explore this issue, table 7A2.1 reports treatment group impacts for men from each site based on three impact regressions:

1. A model that used the full analytic sample and did not include layoff-job wage as an independent variable
2. A model that used the subsample for which layoff-job wage rates were available, but did not include this variable
3. A model that included layoff-job wage rate and used only the layoff wage subsample.

Consider what happens as one shifts from the full sample to the layoff-wage subsample without including layoff wage in the model (columns one and two). Note the increase from $739 to $1,322 in the annual earnings gain for SER/JOBS I/II, the increase from 0.9 to 2.0 weeks in the six-month employment gain for TEC/HCC I/II, and the decrease from $142 to $98 in the 30-week UI benefit reduction for SER/JOBS I/II.

Even though few of these findings are statistically significant, their point estimates imply major substantive differences produced by shifting from the full experimental sample to the layoff-wage subsample. Because the experimental sample was produced by random assignment and the layoff-wage subsample is an unknown subset of the experimental sample, one should use the full sample for impact estimates unless layoff wages make a major difference when included in the impact regression.

Even if layoff-job wages make a large difference, it is still not clear whether to use full-sample findings that draw on random assignment but do not control for layoff wage, or to use layoff-wage subsample findings that control explicitly for this factor but do not have the methodological advantages produced by random assignment. This dilemma reflects the fact that the layoff-wage subsample could be far more biased than the full experimental sample.

Table 7A2.1
**Impact Estimates With and Without Layoff Wage Rate
in the Regression for Male Treatment Group Members**

	Full sample without layoff wage	Layoff wage sample	
		Without layoff wage	With layoff wage
Annual earnings ($)			
TEC/HCC I	403	230	68
TEC/HCC I/II	320	52	−72
SEE I/II	509	411	504
SER/JOBS I/II	739	1,322	1,299
Weeks worked			
TEC/HCC I	3.0**	3.8**	3.9**
TEC/HCC I/II	0.9	2.0*	2.0*
SEE I/II	1.0	1.3	1.3
SER/JOBS I/II	0.0	−0.1	−0.1
30-week UI benefits ($)			
TEC/HCC I	−145	−128	−162
TEC/HCC I/II	−119	−157	−172
SEE I/II	−185	−132	−122
SER/JOBS I/II	−142	−98	−105

* or **=statistically significant at the 0.05 or 0.01 level, one-tail.

Columns two and three in the table indicate that including layoff wage in the impact regression did not produce a major difference. Indeed, including this variable made far less difference than the shift in sample composition required to do so. Given the potential danger of limiting the sample to persons with layoff-wage data and the minimal benefits of controlling for this variable, it was not controlled for explicitly in the impact analysis. Even if it had been, however, the conclusion about Tier I Only versus Tier I/II impacts would be the same.

Appendix 7.3
Sample Sizes for Subgroup Analyses

Tables 7A3.1–7A3.3 present sample sizes for the subgroup analyses presented in tables 7.9, 7.10, and 7.11. Note that sample sizes for different subgroup definitions do not add to the same total because the variables upon which subgroups are based have different numbers of missing cases.

Table 7A3.1
Sample Sizes for Houston Male Subgroup Analyses

| Subgroup | Impact analysis | | |
	Earnings	Weeks worked	UI benefits
Dropout	43	30	54
HS graduate	642	573	772
Under 35	247	211	304
35 plus	438	392	522
Blue-collar	252	229	318
White-collar	408	349	471
Low prior wage	219	211	292
High prior wage	239	220	282
Short prior job	212	199	279
Long prior job	230	217	279
Brief unemployment	392	352	478
Lengthy unemployment	293	251	348

Table 7A3.2
Sample Sizes for El Paso Male Subgroup Analyses

Subgroup	Impact analysis		
	Earnings	Weeks worked	UI benefits
Dropout	198	199	263
HS graduate	160	152	211
Under 35	194	187	260
35 plus	164	164	214
Blue-collar	237	227	308
White-collar	49	51	71
Low prior wage	157	161	209
High prior wage	139	144	195
Short prior job	135	151	202
Long prior job	156	148	197
Brief unemployment	221	236	308
Lengthy unemployment	137	115	166

Table 7A3.3
Sample Sizes for El Paso Female Subgroup Analyses

Subgroup	Impact analysis		
	Earnings	Weeks worked	UI benefits
Dropout	321	318	415
HS graduate	140	136	177
Under 35	235	228	292
35 plus	226	226	300
Blue-collar	381	367	477
White-collar	54	54	77
Low prior wage	209	214	274
High prior wage	193	185	250
Short prior job	198	199	256
Long prior job	198	194	260
Brief unemployment	370	357	468
Lengthy unemployment	91	97	124

8
Summary and Conclusions

This final chapter summarizes the Worker Adjustment Demonstration experience. Specifically, it highlights key implementation issues; summarizes target group characteristics, participation rates, and service receipt patterns; reviews program impacts; and compares these impacts to program costs.

Implementing the Demonstration

Three of the five Worker Adjustment Demonstration sites conducted successful randomized experiments. One initial site dropped out because of conflicting signals and expectations about evaluation requirements, especially the need for random assignment. A second dropped out due to a large infusion of funds for additional local displaced worker programs that would have made equivalent services available to control group members.

The three sites that ran to completion—TEC/HCC in Houston and SEE and SER/JOBS in El Paso—represented different labor markets, different programs, and different types of participants; hence, their findings reflect a broad range of conditions.

Each site's random assignment model varied in complexity, and thus in the impact estimates it could provide. Most complex was the TEC/HCC model, which randomly assigned eligible applicants to three groups:

1. Tier I Only job-search assistance
2. Tier I/II job-search plus occupational training
3. Control status

This model produced internally valid experimental estimates of the net impact of Tier I Only, the net impact of Tier I/II, and the difference between these impacts for comparable individuals. The two-group ex-

159

perimental model at SEE and SER/JOBS randomly assigned eligible applicants to Tier I/II treatment or control status. This furnished internally valid Tier I/II net impact estimates.

Relative to prior randomized field studies, the Worker Adjustment Demonstration was moderately large. Its total research sample of 2,192 persons included 1,366 men and 826 women (1,408 treatment group members and 784 controls). Given the distribution of sample members across sites (1,026 at TEC/HCC, 530 at SEE, and 636 at SER/JOBS), site-specific impact estimates, in addition to average impact estimates, were possible.

Random assignment was conducted by the evaluation contractor with close cooperation from local staff. Crossover rates—the percentage of control group members who received program services—were less than 3 percent. No-show rates—the percentage of treatment group members who did not participate—averaged 29 percent. Hence, the overwhelming majority of experimental sample members received their assigned treatment. Therefore, treatment contrasts were quite sharp and the statistical precision of impact estimates was as strong as possible, given the available sample and program design.

Data for the analysis were obtained from several sources. Program applications were used to determine sample background characteristics. Unemployment insurance records, maintained by the state, were used to measure baseline and follow-up earnings, employment, and UI benefits. A brief telephone follow-up survey—administered one year after random assignment—was used to measure follow-up employment and earnings. On-site analysts and a local respondent network were used to monitor demonstration progress, and to document factors that influenced its success.

UI outcome records were obtained for 97 percent of the persons who went through random assignment, and follow-up surveys were obtained for 74 percent. Total costs to obtain and analyze this information were less than $500,000, spent over two-and-one-half years. On balance then, the Texas Worker Adjustment Demonstration illustrated the feasibility of conducting a high-quality randomized field experiment at several sites simultaneously, within a modest budget and a limited time frame.

Target Groups, Enrollment Rates, and Services Received

Reflecting the major differences in their local economies and populations, the Houston and El Paso projects provided different services to different types of displaced workers.

- *Houston* sample members were overwhelmingly well-educated, highly-paid, white-collar, white males, and were, in large part, laid-off petrochemical workers.
- *El Paso* sample members were overwhelmingly Hispanic, low-wage, poorly-educated, blue-collar workers, and were, in large part, laid-off workers from apparel manufacturing and food processing plants. Men and women were represented equally.

Roughly 60 to 90 percent of all treatment group members received some program services. Participation rates were much higher in El Paso, where the intake process was quicker, more centralized, and had fewer motivational hurdles between random assignment and program participation. SEE and SER/JOBS called in UI referrals directly to their demonstration office for orientation, application, and eligibility determination. Random assignment was conducted within a few days thereafter by the evaluation contractor, and individuals were informed of its outcome immediately. Hence, there were few steps and little time for dropoff to occur between random assignment and program participation. Particularly noteworthy was the 87 percent participation rate achieved by the unusually aggressive SER/JOBS recruitment and retention effort.

TEC/HCC participation rates were somewhat lower (58 to 65 percent) due to the multiple steps, several locations, and consequent time lags in the intake process. Application and eligibility determination were conducted at four local UI offices, after which random assignment was conducted by the evaluation contractor. Sample members were informed of their assignment status within about a week, and treatment group members were referred to the demonstration office for orientation prior to beginning Tier I.

Participants were neither systematically *better-off* nor *worse-off* than no-shows, but there was a tendency for participation to increase with the degree to which programs matched applicants' backgrounds. In addition, the more diverse the applicant pool, the greater the margin for participant and no-show sorting by background characteristics. Furthermore, the more narrowly focused the program, the stronger the tendency for sorting to occur.

Services received by participants varied substantially across sites. These variations reflected treatment group characteristics, hence their needs and capabilities. Services also reflected the prevailing mix of local activities and the institutional backgrounds of each site.

SER/JOBS focused mostly on job-search assistance, and therefore provided Tier II services to only one quarter of its Tier I/II participants. Almost all of this Tier II activity was in the form of OJT. Only 3 percent of SER/JOBS participants received classroom training. This outcome reflected the site's strong emphasis on immediate, income-generating reemployment.

In contrast, TEC/HCC emphasized classroom training for Tier II, reflecting the institutional orientation of Houston Community College. But this training, which was geared to blue-collar occupations, did not match the mainly white-collar backgrounds of TEC/HCC participants. The few OJT slots that were used provided bus drivers for the local transportation authority.

SEE used Tier II services for the greatest proportion of its participants, and provided the most balanced mix of these services—half classroom training and half OJT.

Enrollment durations at each site reflected their service mix; hence, Tier II participants were enrolled longer than Tier I participants.

Program Impacts

The primary goal of the demonstration was to provide valid estimates of program impacts on future earnings, employment, and UI benefits. To address this issue, estimates were developed for the following:

1. The impact of being *offered* program services, referred to as *treatment group impacts*

2. The impact of actually *receiving* program services, referred to as *participant impacts*

Both types of impact measures tell the same basic story. To summarize these findings, table 8.1 presents average *participant* impacts for all men in the sample, and women from the El Paso sites. Impacts for women from Houston were not included, because their treatment and control samples were not sufficiently comparable to provide valid estimates.

Table 8.1
Summary of Participant Impacts

Impact	All men		El Paso women	
Earnings	**Dollars**	**Percent**	**Dollars**	**Percent**
1st UI quarter	104	7	480**	93**
2nd UI quarter	470*	26*	431**	45**
3rd UI quarter	4	<1	288**	28**
4th UI quarter	94	4	−52	−6
Annual	673	8	1,148**	34**
Survey week	−10	−4	17*	19*
Employment				
Percent employed				
1st UI quarter		3		23**
2nd UI quarter		4		14**
3rd UI quarter		−5		12**
4th UI quarter		−5		−3
Weeks worked				
3rd survey quarter		1.3**		1.8**
4th survey quarter		0.3		1.1*
UI benefits				
Percent on UI				
Week 10		−8*		−20**
Week 20		−5		−10**
Week 30		−1		− 7**
	Dollars	**Percent**	**Dollars**	**Percent**
30-week benefits	−207*	−13*	−227**	−19**

* or **=statistically significant at the 0.05 or 0.01 level, one-tail.

First, consider program impacts for El Paso women. During the first three quarters after random assignment, female participants' earnings were increased by $480 (93 percent), $431 (45 percent), and $288 (28 percent) beyond what they would have been, if they had not participated. Fourth-quarter findings are difficult to interpret because of probable data reporting problems. Nevertheless, during the year after random assignment, female participants experienced a total program-induced earnings gain of $1,148 (34 percent). Furthermore, during the follow-up survey week, one year after random assignment, they experienced a $17 (19 percent) weekly earnings gain.

These earnings gains were mirrored by employment gains of 23, 14, and 12 percentage points, during the first three UI follow-up quarters. Once again, fourth-quarter UI data were difficult to interpret. But survey responses indicate that employment gains for women—expressed as increased weeks worked during their third and fourth follow-up quarters— were substantial (1.8 and 1.1 weeks, respectively).

Corresponding UI benefit impacts were also quite large. During weeks 10, 20, and 30 after random assignment, female participants experienced a 20, 10, and 7 percentage-point reduction in their likelihood of receiving UI benefits. Their total 30-week benefit reduction averaged $227 (19 percent). Hence, the demonstration produced large early impacts for women. These impacts diminished gradually, but probably persisted beyond the one-year follow-up period for the study.

Impacts for men were quite different. Their earnings gains were pronounced ($470, or 26 percent) only during the second follow-up quarter, and their total annual gain, $673 (8 percent), was half that for women. By the end of the first year after random assignment, there was no remaining impact. Nevertheless, a sizeable UI benefit reduction ($207, or 13 percent) was realized during their first 30 weeks after random assignment. In short, the demonstration produced an early but short-lived reemployment boost for men.

The random assignment model implemented by TEC/HCC also made possible a comparison of Tier I Only versus Tier I/II impacts. This analysis (table 7.5) suggested no increase in impacts from the addition of Tier II occupational skills training. However, the blue-collar orientation of TEC/HCC Tier II activities did not match the predominantly white-collar backgrounds of its participants. Hence, as noted in chapter 7, TEC/HCC findings do not prove that supplementing job-search assistance with occupational skills training cannot be effective; they simply indicate that this approach was not effective at TEC/HCC, given the mismatch between its Tier II offerings and participants' backgrounds.

A final important set of impact findings were produced by comparing estimates for sample subgroups, defined in terms of their education, age, prior occupation, prior wage rate, prior job length, and duration of unemployment. This analysis suggested that better-educated, more highly-paid white-collar workers benefited most from the TEC/HCC program, or at least its Tier I job-search component, which was geared toward white-collar professionals. In contrast, blue-collar, lower-paid, school dropouts experienced negative impacts. This finding underscores the importance of matching a program to its target group.

Impacts Versus Costs

Worker Adjustment Demonstration impacts cannot be evaluated fully without considering program costs. Thus table 8.2 compares participant impacts on earnings and UI benefits with estimated program costs per participant.[1] A more comprehensive benefit-cost analysis was not feasible, given limited project resources. Nevertheless, the simple comparison of costs and impacts presented below tells a rather striking story.

Two cost measures were developed for each site. One measured the average cost of providing the service mix received by Tier I/II participants. The second measured average Tier I costs per participant. Both were based on budget data from the sites and a range of assumptions that reflect the relationship between Tier I and Tier II costs implied by findings from prior research (Jerret et al. 1983; Levitan and Mangum 1981; Zornitsky 1984; Wegman 1979). Appendix 8.1 describes how these estimates were obtained.[2]

Table 8.2 indicates that average Tier I costs were between $1,460 and $2,072 at TEC/HCC, between $407 and $702 at SEE, and between $406 and $574 at SER/JOBS. The low cost of Tier I at SEE and

SER/JOBS reflects its limited duration (one week), the inexpensive facilities used, and the probable low overhead for these small, centralized, in-house programs. The high cost of Tier I at TEC/HCC reflects its longer duration and greater intensity (two weeks of instruction followed by four weeks of supervised job-search), its more elaborate facilities (located in an exclusive shopping mall), and higher costs probably required to administer this more complex multisite, multiorganizational program.

Table 8.2
Participant Impacts and Costs
(Dollars)

Participant impacts	Earnings		UI benefits
Houston men	547		−204
El Paso men	770		−194
El Paso women	1,148**		−227**
Participant costs	**Assumption A**	**Assumption B**	**Assumption C**
Tier I			
TEC/HCC	2,072	1,713	1,460
SEE	702	515	407
SER/JOBS	574	475	406
Tier I/II			
TEC/HCC	2,981	3,215	3,381
SEE	1,099	1,099	1,099
SER/JOBS	725	725	725

NOTE: Assumption A: Tier II=Tier I costs; Assumption B: Tier II=two times Tier I costs; Assumption C: Tier II=three times Tier I costs.
**=statistically significant at the 0.01 level, one-tail. No significant findings were significant at only the 0.05 level.

Average Tier I/II costs were $725 at SER/JOBS, $1,099 at SEE, and $2,981 to $3,381 at TEC/HCC. To place these costs in perspective, note that average national JTPA Title III costs were $904 in program year 1985 (U.S. General Accounting Office 1990). The especially low Tier I/II cost at SER/JOBS reflects the site's lower costs and minimal Tier II enrollment (only 26 percent of Tier I/II participants got Tier II services). In contrast, the high Tier I/II cost at TEC/HCC reflects the site's high Tier I cost plus the expense of providing classroom training through Houston Community College.[3] The moderate cost at SEE reflects the brief, open-entry, open-exit, occupational familiarization courses it offered.

A comparison of the preceding costs with program impact estimates presented earlier suggests that programs for women from the two El Paso sites were cost-effective; average Tier I/II costs ranged from $725 to $1,099 per participant, whereas program-induced earnings gains averaged $1,148. In addition, because earnings gains for women appeared to continue beyond the one-year follow-up period for the study, they probably exceeded program costs by more than observation would suggest. Furthermore, from a governmental budgetary perspective, program-induced UI benefit reductions—which averaged $227 per participant—were an offset to program costs; hence, El Paso programs were even more cost-effective for women from this perspective.

Findings for men were less clear, however, On average, earnings gains for male El Paso participants were $770 and UI benefit reductions were $194. Neither finding was statistically significant. Nevertheless, these estimates suggest that earnings gains for El Paso men were slightly less than program costs. Accounting for UI benefit reductions, however, the programs approximately *broke even*.

The Houston program had substantially higher costs but smaller impacts. Its Tier I/II sequence cost between $2,981 and $3,381 per participant and its Tier I Only component cost between $1,460 and $2,072. Program impacts for the two program strategies were roughly the same and averaged $547 in increased earnings and $204 in UI benefit reductions. Hence, neither the Tier I/II nor the Tier I Only treatment stream in Houston was cost-effective.

In summary, the two El Paso programs, whose costs were close to the national JTPA Title III average, were clearly cost-effective for women and marginally cost-effective for men, but the Houston program, which cost several times the national average, was not cost- effective.

Conclusions

On balance, it seems fair to conclude that the Texas Worker Adjustment Demonstration was successful in at least three important regards.

1. *As a social experiment,* it was well-executed and provided a large, high-quality data base from which to study the effectiveness of employment and training services, and the process by which they are provided.
2. *As a program for laid-off workers,* it furnished an important reemployment stimulus that expedited the process by which participants found new jobs, and thereby reduced their dependence on Unemployment Insurance.
3. *As a cost-effective service strategy,* the benefits of programs in two out of three sites equaled or exceeded its costs to the government.

As with any single study, however, the present one is suggestive, not definitive. It can only indicate probable fruitful options, not prove specific points. Nevertheless, its findings comprise a large portion of a small existing research base on a problem of major national significance.

We are now entering a new stage of displaced worker programming in this country, with passage of the Economic Dislocation and Worker Adjustment Assistance Act of 1988 (EDWAA). This new law is intended to change the funding, the state and local institutional structure, the targeting, and the service mix of federally funded displaced worker programs. In addition, local economic displacement caused by reduced military spending from attempts to accrue a *peace dividend* may increase the need for assistance in some communities.

But state and local governments must implement these new initiatives with a limited research base upon which to draw. Thus it is hoped that the present volume will contribute specific information to this effort, and stimulate further rigorous testing of innovations, so that future plans can make better use of past experience.

NOTES

1. Program-induced earnings gains represent a clear benefit for participants. But for society as a whole, they only represent a benefit to the extent that participants' gains are not offset by others' losses. The magnitude of this offset, often referred to as *displacement,* has been the subject of debate for decades. Thus, it remains unclear how much of participants' earnings gains are a social benefit, and how much are a transfer of resources from one group to another. UI benefit reductions are a gain to taxpayers and a loss to participants; hence, from a social perspective, they are a transfer. From the government's budgetary perspective, however, they represent a potentially important offset to program costs.

2. The present method for computing Tier I versus Tier I/II costs differs from that used originally by Bloom and Kulik (1986).

3. Houston Community College was the sole provider of classroom training for TEC/HCC, for which it maintained a full-time, seven-person staff. Due to the mismatch between the mostly white-collar TEC/HCC participants and the mainly blue-collar HCC course offerings, this staff probably was not fully utilized by the demonstration.

Appendix 8.1
Average Program Cost Estimates

Basic Approach

Estimates of average program costs by site and for Tier I versus Tier I/II were based on total cumulative costs and the number of sample members who received Tier I or Tier II services at each site. Total reported program costs were $1,305,538 for TEC/HCC, $230,860 for SEE, and $212,522 for SER/JOBS, according to monthly invoices submitted to TDCA. The numbers of participants who received only Tier I services were 197 for TEC/HCC I, 169 for TEC/HCC I/II, 91 for SEE I/II, and 216 for SER/JOBS I/II. The numbers of participants who received Tier I plus Tier II services were 132 for TEC/HCC I/II, 119 for SEE I/II, and 77 for SER/JOBS I/II. No sample members received only Tier II services.

Estimates of average cost per participant in the SEE and SER/JOBS Tier I/II treatment streams were obtained by dividing total program costs by total participants. This result was $1,099 for SEE and $725 for SER/JOBS, and is reported as average Tier I/II costs in table 8.2.

Tier I/II average costs were more difficult to estimate for TEC/HCC, because the project had separate Tier I and Tier I/II treatment streams, but did not record expenses separately. It was necessary, therefore, to make a range of assumptions about the ratio between Tier I and Tier II costs, and impose these ratios on total cost and participant data. It was then possible to separate Tier I and Tier II costs, given their assumed ratio. The Tier I/II cost estimate for TEC/HCC and the Tier I cost estimates for each site reflect the following assumptions:

Assumption A. Average Tier II costs equal average Tier I costs.
Assumption B. Average Tier II costs equal two times average Tier I costs.
Assumption C. Average Tier II costs equal three times average Tier I costs.

To illustrate the implications of these assumptions, note that if average Tier I costs were $400, then average Tier I plus II costs would be $800 under assumption A, $1,200 under assumption B and $1,600 under assumption C. These assumptions span the range of Tier I versus Tier II cost ratios implied by findings from previous research (Jerret et al. 1983; Levitan and Mangum 1981; Zornitsky 1984; Wegman 1979). Fortunately, the conclusions of the present analysis are not sensitive to these assumptions.

171

Separating Tier I and Tier II Costs

Equations A1 and A2 below were used to impose the preceding assumptions on the cost and participant data for each site. These equations were solved for average Tier I costs, which in turn were used to determine average Tier I/II costs.

$$\text{TOTAL COST} = N_I \cdot \text{COST}_I + N_{II} [\text{COST}_I + \text{COST}_{II}] \qquad [A1]$$

and

$$\text{COST}_{II} = X \cdot \text{COST}_I \qquad [A2]$$

where:

N_I = the number of participants who received only Tier I services;

N_{II} = the number of participants who received Tier II services plus Tier I services;

COST_I = the average cost of Tier I per recipient;

COST_{II} = the average cost of Tier II per recipient;

X = the assumed ratio between Tier II and Tier I average costs ($X=1$, $X=2$ or $X=3$);

TOTAL COST = total program cost.

Substituting Equation A2 into Equation A1 yields:

$$\text{TOTAL COST} = N_I \cdot \text{COST}_I + N_{II} \cdot [X + 1] \cdot \text{COST}_I \qquad [A3]$$

Site-specific values for TOTAL COST, N_I and N_{II}, plus an assumed value for X were input to Equation A3. This produced one linear equation in one unknown, COST_I, which in turn was solved for COST_I, the Tier I cost estimates in table 8.2.

Average cost per TEC/HCC Tier I/II participant were computed based on estimated Tier I average costs, corresponding Tier II average costs, and the actual number of TEC/HCC participants who received Tier I or Tier I plus Tier II services.

References

Abt Associates, and National Opinion Research Corporation. Unpublished response rate tabulations for the JTPA "Full Baseline Experimental" and "Eligible Nonparticipant" baseline surveys for the National JTPA Study. Cambridge, MA: Abt Associates, 1990.

Ashenfelter, Orley. "Estimating the Effect of Training Programs on Earnings." *Review of Economics and Statistics* 61 (February 1979): 47-57.

Bassi, Laurie J. "The Effect of CETA on the Postprogram Earnings of Participants." *Journal of Human Resources* 18 (November 1984): 539-556.

Bendick, Mark Jr., and Judith R. Devine. "Workers Dislocated by Economic Change: Do They Need Federal Employment and Training Assistance?" In *Seventh Annual Report: The Federal Interest in Employment and Training*. Washington D.C.: National Commission for Employment Policy (October 1981): 175-226.

Betsey, Charles L., Robinson Hollister Jr., and Mary R. Papageorgiou, eds. *Youth Employment and Training Programs: The YEDPA Years.* Washington, D.C.: National Academy Press, 1985.

Bloom, Howard S. "Accounting for No-Shows in Experimental Evaluation Designs." *Evaluation Review* 8, 2 (April 1984a): 225-246.

Bloom, Howard S. "Estimating the Effect of Job-Training Programs, Using Longitudinal Data, Ashenfelter's Findings Reconsidered." *The Journal of Human Resources* 19, 4 (Fall 1984b): 544-556.

Bloom, Howard S. "Lessons From the Delaware Dislocated Worker Pilot Program." *Evaluation Review* 11, 2 (April 1987a): 157-177.

Bloom, Howard S. "What Works for Whom? CETA Impacts for Adult Participants." *Evaluation Review* 11, 4 (August 1987b): 510-527.

Bloom, Howard S., and Jane Kulik. *Evaluation of the Worker Adjustment Demonstration: Final Report.* Cambridge, MA: Abt Associates, 1986.

Bloom, Howard S., Jane Kulik, Glen Schneider, and Linda Sharpe. *Worker Adjustment Demonstration Project Evaluation: Design Report.* Cambridge, MA: Abt Associates, 1984.

Bolles, Richard N. *What Color Is Your Parachute? A Practical Manual for Job-Hunters and Career Changes.* Berkeley, CA: Ten Speed Press, 1984.

Borsch-Supan, Axel. *Econometric Analysis of Discrete Choice.* New York: Springer-Verlag, 1987.

Bryant, Edward C., and Kalman Rupp. "Evaluating the Impact of CETA on Participant Earnings." *Evaluation Review* 11 (August 1987): 473-492.

Campbell, Donald, T. "Reforms as Experiments." In *Handbook of Evaluation Research,* 1, edited by Elmer L. Struening and Marcia Guttentag, 71-100. Beverly Hills: Sage Publications, 1975.

Cook, Thomas, and Donald T. Campbell. *Quasi-Experimental Design and Analysis Issues for Field Settings.* Chicago: Rand McNally, 1979.

Corson, Walter, Paul T. Decker, Shari Miller Dunstan, and Anne R. Gordon. *The New Jersey Unemployment Insurance Reemployment Demonstration Project: Final Evaluation Report.* Princeton, NJ: Mathematica Policy Research, 1989.

Corson, Walter, Sharon Long, and Rebecca Maynard. *An Impact Evaluation of the Buffalo Dislocated Worker Demonstration Program.* Princeton, NJ: Mathematica Policy Research, 1985.

Dickinson, Katherine P., Terry R. Johnson, and Richard W. West. "An Analysis of the Impact of CETA Programs on Participants' Earnings." *The Journal of Human Resources* 21 (Winter 1986): 64-91.

Flaim, Paul O., and Ellen Sehgal. "Displaced Workers of 1979-83: How Well Have They Fared?" *Monthly Labor Review* (June 1985): 3-16.

Fraker, Thomas, and Rebecca Maynard. "The Adequacy of Comparison Group Designs for Evaluations of Employment-Related Programs." *The Journal of Human Resources* 22 (Spring 1987): 194-227.

Hausman, Jerry A. and David A. Wise, eds. *Social Experimentation.* Chicago: University of Chicago Press, 1985.

Heckman, James. "Sample Selection Bias as a Specification Error." *Econometrica* 47 (January 1979): 153-161.

Homans, Celia. "Finding the Hard-to-Locate: The NORC Experience." In *Evaluating the Impact of Manpower Programs,* edited by Michael E. Borus, 155-164. Lexington, MA: Lexington Books, D.C. Heath, 1972.

Jastrzab, JoAnn. *Final Report on the Initial Wave of the STEP Survey.* Cambridge, MA: Abt Associates, 1988.

Jastrzab, JoAnn, Jane Kulik, Glen Schneider, and Linda Sharpe. *Worker Adjustment Demonstration Project Evaluation: Formative Evaluation Report.* Cambridge, MA: Abt Associates, 1984.

Jerret, Marcia, et al. *Serving the Dislocated Worker: A Report on the Dislocated Worker Demonstration Program.* Cambridge, MA: Abt Associates, 1983.

Kiefer, Nicholas M. "Population Heterogeneity and Inference from Panel Data on the Effects of Vocational Education." *Journal of Political Economy* 87 (October 1979): S213-26.

Kulik, Jane and Linda Sharpe. *Worker Adjustment Demonstration Project Evaluation: Comparative Evaluation Report.* Cambridge, MA: Abt Associates, 1985.

Kulik, Jane, D. Alton Smith, and Ernst Stromsdorfer. *The Downriver Community Conference Economic Readjustment Program: Final Evaluation Report.* Cambridge, MA: Abt Associates, 1984.

LaLonde, R.J. "Evaluating the Econometric Evaluations of Training Programs with Experimental Data." *American Economic Review* 76 (September 1986): 604-620.

LaLonde, R.J., and Rebecca Maynard. "How Precise Are Evaluations of Employment and Training Programs: Evidence from a Field Experiment." *Evaluation Review* 11 (August 1987): 428-451.

Levitan, Sar A., and Garth L. Mangum. *The T in CETA: Local and National Perspectives.* Kalamazoo, MI: W.E. Upjohn Institute for Employment Research, 1981.

Myers, Brooks. *A Comparison of the Unemployment Insurance Benefit Systems in Texas and Selected States.* Austin, TX: Texas Employment Commission, 1989.

National Opinion Research Corporation. *High School and Beyond 1980 Senior Cohort Third Followup, 1986: Volume II Users Manual.* University of Chicago (October 1987).

Pindyck, Robert S., and Daniel L. Rubinfeld. *Econometric Models and Economic Forecasts.* New York: McGraw-Hill, 1976.

Riecken, Henry W., and Robert F. Boruch. *Social Experimentation: A Method for Planning and Evaluating Social Interventions.* New York: Academic Press, 1974.

Secretary of Labor's Task Force on Economic Adjustment and Worker Dislocation. *Economic Adjustment and Worker Dislocation in a Competitive Society.* Washington, D.C. (December 1986).

Sheingold, Steven. *Dislocated Workers: Issues and Federal Options.* Washington, D.C.: U.S. Congressional Budget Office, 1982.

Stromsdorfer, Ernst et al. *Recommendations of the Job Training Longitudinal Survey Research Advisory Panel.* Washington, D.C.: U.S. Department of Labor, Employment and Training Administration, 1985.

U.S. Congressional Budget Office. *Summary of the Economic Effects of Reduced Defense Spending* (March 1990).

U.S. Department of Labor, Division of Performance Management and Evaluation, Office of Strategic Planning and Policy Development. *Summary of JTQS Data for JTPA Title IIA and III Enrollments and Terminations During PY 1987* (December 1988).

U.S. General Accounting Office. *Dislocated Workers: Expenditures Under Title III of the Job Training Partnership Act.* 1990.

U.S. House of Representatives. *Job Training Partnership Act.* Conference Report 97-889.

Wegman, Robert G. "Job-Search Assistance: A Review." *Journal of Employment Counseling* 16 (December 1979).

Zornitsky, Jeffrey et al. *Measuring the Costs of JTPA Program Participation.* Cambridge, MA: Abt Associates, 1984.

Index

Abt Associates, Inc., 5-6, 16-17, 53n3
Ashenfelter, Orly, 110

Bassi, Laurie J., 28, 41, 67, 110
Bendick, Mark, Jr., 70
Betsey, Charles L., 28, 33
Bloom, Howard S., 6, 25n12, 28, 40, 41, 67, 89, 110, 169n2
Bolles, Richard N., 24n8
Borsch-Supan, Axel, 131
Boruch, Robert F., 6, 28
Bryant, Edward C., 28, 110

Cameron County Private Industry Council, 5
Campbell, Donald T., 42n3
Career Circles, 12, 13, 24n8, 90, 144
Corson, Walter, 25n12, 89
Cost measures, 165-67

Data: follow-up surveys to collect, 55-60; requirements of, 43-45; sources for, 45-53, 107-9, 160
Devine, Judith R., 70
Dickinson, Katherine P., 28, 110
Displaced worker programs: effect of offering services, 131-37; effect of receiving program services, 139-47; under JTPA Title III, 3; participation rates in Buffalo and Delaware, 89-90
Displaced workers: client assessment for participants, 12-13; criteria for identifying, 70-72; development and implementation of adjustment programs for, 7-16; job-search assistance for, 13-15; JTPA guidelines to identify, 70-72; retraining of, 15-16; *See also* Worker Adjustment Demonstration

Earnings: decline and similarity in preprogram, 110-14; differentiation between male and female, 114-15; effect of offering program services on, 135, 136; unemployment insurance reported as, 115
Economic Dislocation and Worker Adjustment Assistance Act of 1988 (EDWAA), 168
Eligibility: prior employment as requirement for, 115; and probability of participation, 34, 87
El Paso labor market, 17-24
El Paso School for Educational Enrichment (SEE): baseline earnings for participants in, 110-14; characteristics of sample of participants, 67-70, 73, 82; client assessment by, 12-13; comparison of treatment and control group earnings, 128-29; cost measures for, 165-67; effect of labor market conditions on, 18-24; enrollment for, 103-4; funding, tiers and sites for, 5-7, 8; job-search assistance (Tier I) by, 14, 96-103; participant and no-show characteristics for, 93-96; participation rates for, 91; program services for displaced workers in, 161-62; random assignment model of, 29-31, 32, 159-60; recruitment process for, 10; retraining (Tier II), 16, 96-103; services received by participants in, 96-103; targets to obtain clients, 10-12
Emergencies Jobs Bill, 5
Employment. *See* El Paso labor market; Houston labor market; Labor market conditions: comparison of treatment and control groups for, 115-19; effect of offering program services on, 135, 136

177